Stanley Parker received his MSc in 1964 and his PhD in 1968, both from London University. He is a research Officer at the Government Social Survey, specialising in research on industrial and labour matters. He is the joint author of *The Sociology of Industry* (1967).

The Future

Stanley Parker

# of Work and Leisure

Paladin

Granada Publishing Limited
Published in 1972 by Paladin
3 Upper James Street, London W1R 4BP

First published by MacGibbon & Kee Ltd 1971
Copyright © S. R. Parker 1971
Made and printed in Great Britain by
Hazell Watson & Viney Ltd,
Aylesbury, Bucks.
Set in Monotype Ehrhardt

Contents

Acknowledgements

THE SUBJECT of work and leisure first started to interest me when I attended the postgraduate sociology seminars at the Regent Street Polytechnic, London from 1962 to 1965. The sociology of occupations was one of the focal points of these seminars and my segment of the subject became work and leisure – partly because it seemed worthwhile and partly because no one else was specializing in it. To Stephen Cotgrove who organized the seminars and to the other members I am indebted for many stimulating discussions and valuable 'feedback' to my early ideas on the subject.

Most of the research reported in Chapter 7 grew out of the seminars and out of my study of the research and ideas of previous writers, many of whom are referred to in footnotes throughout the book. Edna and Jim Mathieson and Kate Danziger helped with some of the interviewing – my thanks to them and to all the people who took part in the surveys. Part of the cost of the research was met by a grant from the University of London Central Research Fund.

I wish warmly to thank Louis Moss, of the Government Social Survey, for help and encouragement in using some of the data from the Survey of Local Government Councillors. For permission to quote this data I am grateful to the Director of the Department. As one of its employees, I must state that the views expressed in this book are those of the author and do not represent the views of the Government Social Survey.

I have tried never to lose an opportunity of discussing the subject of this book with any group I have been in contact with. At sociological conferences, student meetings, mixed groups of shop stewards and managers, there have usually been people from whom I have got a new slant on the subject or criticism which made me re-think my ideas.

More personal acknowledgements fall into two groups. There

Acknowledgements

are those whose own research projects are at least partly in the field of work and leisure and with whom I have exchanged ideas and information: Jan Arriens, Bill Bacon, Terence Chivers, John Crutchley, Michael Smith and Donald Swift. Others not so involved, but who have nevertheless had an influence on this book in various ways, include: Richard Brown, John Child, Raymond Firth, John Goldthorpe, Max Kaplan, John McGregor, John Rowan, Malcolm Stott and Roger Thomas.

This book incorporates the substance of a thesis which was approved by the University of London for the award of the degree of Doctor of Philosophy. My special thanks are due to John Rex who, as managing editor of this series, offered much practical and detailed advice on how to turn the thesis into what we both hope is a more readable book.

S. R. P.

The Future of Work and Leisure

1 Introduction

We hear quite a lot these days about the 'problem of leisure'. We hear less about the problem of work. Yet both are really part of the same problem, and a careful consideration of all the issues involved shows that we are unlikely to go far in solving the one without tackling the other. The *quantity* of leisure time is increasing for many people – although not at such a dramatic rate as some observers would have us believe – because working time is getting less. Shorter working weeks, longer holidays, a longer period of retirement because we tend to give up work earlier and live longer – all these things are giving us more leisure. Not everyone, however, is participating in this leisure boom. People in some occupations are finding that work is as demanding as ever. It is the people who find work most absorbing who have least leisure, whereas those in more or less routine jobs – who, according to some commentators, have the least resources for using leisure time creatively – are finding more time on their hands.

Of course the experiences of work and leisure by individual people have to be looked at against the social and economic background of the larger community of which they are part. Faced with the choice of more leisure time or more income, a good many British workers still choose more income from overtime, a second job, or do-it-yourself activities which are hardly leisure. This is mainly because the income from a basic working week at many jobs is still too low to afford a decent standard of living. The time will come, however, when the development of automation and other technological progress will mean that the choice between more work and more leisure need no longer be dictated by economic necessity. We may grumble about certain aspects of our jobs, but it is only when we are forced to retire that many of us realize how big a part the job played in our lives. Those of us who are lucky enough to be employed in doing the kind of work that we should choose to do even if we were financially free would not need to make such a big adjustment – the end of employment would not mean the end of *work* of a kind we thought worthwhile. But others among us who are denied the opportunity of working in this way may well find that too much leisure is an even bigger problem than too much work.

Some people look on leisure and work in the same way as the hedonist philosophy looks on pleasure and pain – the one to be eagerly sought after and the other to be avoided like the plague. But experts in the various social sciences agree that both work *and* leisure are necessary to a healthy life and a healthy society, though whether these two spheres need to be as separate as they are for most people today is debatable. The idea that work cannot be made a source of interest and even fulfilment for the mass of people, and therefore that we should pin our hopes on leisure, is as one-sided as the view that work is the real business of life and that leisure is just a waste of time. Maximum human development in both work and leisure spheres requires that they be complementary rather than that one be regarded as 'good' and the other 'bad'.

To the extent that we *do* think of work as something unpleasant and to be avoided this is usually because of the purpose for which it is done or the conditions under which it is done. If the purpose of work is simply to earn money in order to live, then both the employee and his employer tend to ignore the possibility of making work itself a meaningful experience. Even trade unions – who claim to look after the interests of workers – largely ignore the possibility of making the experience of work more worthwhile in itself, while struggling to make it more remunerative and less time consuming This is typical of a society in which we have become used to the idea of exploiting human resources along with other resources. We may say that things are different when it comes to leisure. But life is of a piece, and people who are accustomed to being exp oited in their work may find it hard to avoid being exploited in heir leisure.

*

So we arrive at the proposition that the problem of leisure is also the problem of work. This doesn't mean that there is nothing we can do to improve leisure opportunities quite apart from anything we may do about the organization of work. The need for better facilities for different types of leisure activity is widely recognized, and as our productivity improves we shall no doubt be able to afford to spend a larger proportion of the national income on leisure goods and services. But that would be only to tackle the material side of things. There is some evidence that the people who are the least involved in their work are also the least involved in their leisure – that frustration in one sphere goes along with frustration in another. To expect a change in one part of life which would not affect other parts is to assume a split that is not easy to make or to sustain, even if it is thought desirable.

It is tempting to believe that whatever differences there are between what people put into and get out of work and leisure are the result of their personalities or 'the sort of people they are'. Because people who think like this discount the effects of environment, they advocate that we should try to match 'types of person' to 'types of situation'. They overlook the possibility that, at least to some extent, people are shaped, changed, developed or retarded by the types of situation they are put into. But if we put people into categories at the beginning of their adult lives – if we say that some need work into which they can put a lot of themselves, while others need only a satisfying leisure life – then we are restricting their range of opportunities for a full and balanced life.

A programme designed to realize human potentialities would have both a work and a leisure aspect. In the work sphere, employees, individually or through their unions or other associations, can demand more interesting work and a greater say in how it is organized. The apathy of many workers and the reluctance of management to let workers have a say in how things are run are obstacles to be overcome, but experiments in a few progressive enterprises show what can be done on a wider scale. A revaluation of leisure would need to complement such a revaluation of work. To most people, leisure means time during which they feel free to do whatever they want to. Consequently it is thought to be wrong for a society to attempt to plan the leisure of its members. Up to a point we can, of course, choose to do what we like in our free time, but somehow we manage to spend much of our time and money as customers of one or another branch of the leisure industry, which is organized on the same lines as most factories and offices. If we are not encouraged to think for ourselves at school and at work, we are not likely to have the mental resources to think for ourselves in leisure time.

*

This book is a study of the relationship between man at work and man at play. It has both theoretical and practical aims: to contribute to the development of sociological theory, including evaluating alternative views of man, society and social change; and to contribute to the solution of problems of work and leisure, by attempting to predict the likely outcome of alternative social policies.

In order to understand our present social situation and its possible future development, we need to know something of the past and of other cultures besides our own. In this book I shall adopt what may be called a 'sociological perspective', while recognizing that the subject of work and leisure lends itself to approaches other than the sociological one. Psychology enters into it because how people relate their work to their leisure or seek to separate these two spheres is to some extent a matter for individual choice. History and anthropology have something to contribute because meanings of work and leisure have changed through the ages and are even today different in various cultures. Philosophy and religion have a stake in this area because the quality and values of 'the good life' certainly involve some conception of how work and leisure make their separate or joint contributions to it. Social planning, too, is concerned – indeed, those of us who claim to be applied rather than merely theoretical sociologists may see the aim of all our knowledge as a contribution to the solution of social problems.

Sociology is concerned with relationships, and there are two types of relationship to be studied: that between society's need for work to be done and for the benefits that its members may collectively derive from leisure; and that between the functions of work and leisure to individuals themselves. The prevailing values attached to leisure must bear some relationship to the values attached to work, since for most people in present society leisure is only possible after work has first been done. Apart from any theoretical interest in the social and individual relationships involved in work and leisure, there is also a more practical concern about 'the problem of leisure', which, as I hope to show, in the long run also involves the problem of work. Some knowledge about the actual relationship between work and leisure in past and present societies should help us to predict what forms this relationship might take, given certain changes in the structure of society and/or in the prevailing set of values.

It is important to recognize the nature of the problems facing policy makers in this field. Like all planners, they are concerned with establishing priorities and reconciling divergent interests. They *should* be trying to steer a course between *laissez-faire* and authoritarianism, between letting things take their own way (often a way determined by vested interests) and seeking to control people's lives from the cradle to the grave. The experience of working life is not usually thought of as a social problem. There is plenty of justified concern about helping people to get a job, training them for it, making conditions in it hygienic and safe for them, and (more recently) compensating them if they lose it. But seldom is anything said about whether it is a job fit for human beings to do, whether it develops them as persons, whether it gives them anything beyond the pay packet and a feeling that time at work is time wasted. There is more interest in 'the problem of leisure', but too often this is defined narrowly as a problem only for certain minority groups such as teenagers or retired persons. The rest of us may not realize that we have a problem until we are shown a solution – that is, the steps that are required to change society so that more people are afforded more opportunities for a creative and satisfying work and leisure life.

*

It is only partly true to say that the subject of work and leisure has been neglected in discussions of what sort of society we are trying to build. The theme of work *as production* is often in the news. It is said that British people do not work hard enough compared with people in other countries or with the 'good old days' in this country; that management by and large doesn't know how to organize production efficiently; that it is still possible (or not possible) for people to 'get to the top' from humble beginnings by hard work, and so on. But the ways in which leisure enagages the public attention are on a different plane altogether. It is said that what we need are more leisure facilities, more ways of filling our free time, that our children should be educated for leisure as well as – or even rather than – for work, and our older people educated in how to cope with retirement after a lifetime of employment.

Only rarely, however, are the problems of work and leisure looked at *together*. Sometimes an individual pauses in his daily round of activity to assess the balance of his own life, to take stock and plan for the future. In the following pages we shall be looking at our *society* in this way; not at the whole of it (that would take many more pages) but at every aspect of the relationship between work and leisure. We shall draw on the researches and thoughts of many people who have had something to say on these matters.

At the outset it may help the reader to see the relevance of these studies to his own concern with work and leisure if they are briefly reviewed in terms of what their particular interests are. *First*, there are the attempts to sort out what is meant by work and leisure in the pattern of life – no easy task, because there is much loose thinking and confusion in this field. *Secondly*, research into how people in societies other than our own relate the work and leisure parts of their lives – or whether, indeed, they make such a distinction at all – helps to put our own behaviour and ideas into perspective. *Thirdly*, there are different kinds of work and different kinds of leisure in our modern industrial society and we can learn a lot from surveys of how people in various circumstances tend to behave in and think about work and leisure. *Fourthly*, we have the theorists and philosophers who link definitions and concepts to people and situations and produce ideas about what work and leisure ought to be. *Finally*, the social planners try to find out what people's needs for work and leisure are and put forward programmes designed to meet these needs.

All of these types of study contribute in one way or another to the form that society takes and by knowing about them and taking part in the ongoing discussion of what they mean in our own lives each of us can help to shape our collective future.

2 Problems of Definition

One of the difficulties of the English language is that words like 'work' and 'leisure' have such a wide variety of meanings. The *Oxford Dictionary* takes four columns to list the various usages of 'work' and gives a shorter, but still by no means clear, explanation of what 'leisure' is. It is tempting to argue that since the present words are used to mean so many different things it would be better to abandon them and to start from scratch with new terms which could be clearly defined. But we should still at some points have to translate these new terms back into their old equivalents, and probably this would, on balance, lead to even greater confusion. Our first task, then, is to sort out the various meanings of work and leisure, and to see how they relate to each other.

Definitions of Work

To the individual in a modern industrial society such as ours, work is usually identified with the means of earning a living. In simpler societies the relationship between work and such basic necessities as food, clothing and shelter is a direct one for the individual or for a comparatively small group; they consume only what they are able to produce. The evolution of society through various forms of social production and ownership of property progressively breaks down the direct link between individual productive effort and consumption of goods and services. Hard physical labour is less and less required as machines take over more of the tasks of production. Fewer people are needed to produce the basic necessities of life, and the goods and services of what are sometimes called the 'leisure industries' account for an increasing proportion of total production and employment.

It will be noticed that we have already used, besides work itself, four of its synonyms: production, effort, labour and employment.

Sometimes the adjective 'productive' precedes 'work', but a too literal interpretation of 'productive' is misleading, since the *effort* to produce something is work irrespective of whether a 'product' results, and the rendering of services, no less than the production of goods, requires work. The distinction between the terms work, labour and employment is even more important. Only the last of these terms implies a social relationship, although it is sometimes used in the same non-social sense as work, for example, when we say that someone is 'self-employed'. The most common form of employment consists of an employer (individual or corporate body) hiring the working abilities of an employee during set hours. For the employee, this is the equivalent of *working time*, and it is relatively easy for him to distinguish this from *non-working time*, a part or the whole of which may be defined as leisure.

The other two concepts of work and labour have to do with *activity* rather than time. Both are often equated with employment, but while it is true that all employment implies work of some kind, the reverse is not necessarily so. Employment is work in the narrow sense of income-producing activity, but work has a wider biological and physiological meaning of purposeful and sustained action. Whereas employment may be contrasted with idleness or with work that is economically unremunerative or disinterested, work in its broad meaning is the opposite of rest.

Although 'labour' is often used as a synonym for work, Hannah Arendt has suggested that there is good reason for keeping the two concepts separate. She uses 'labour' to denote necessary activity assuring the survival of the individual and the species, and 'work' to denote an unnatural activity providing an 'artificial' world of things. She maintains that the necessity of 'making a living' (i.e. employment) has reduced nearly all human activities to the level of labour:

Whatever we do, we are supposed to do for the sake of 'making a living'; such is the verdict of society, and the number of people, especially in the professions, who might challenge it has decreased rapidly. The only exception society is willing to grant is the artist who, strictly speaking, is the only 'worker' left in a labouring society. The same trend to level down all serious activities to the status of making a living is manifest in present-day labour theories, which almost unanimously define labour as the opposite of play. As a result, all serious activities, irrespective of their fruits, are called labour, and every activity which is not necessary either for the life of the individual or for the life process of society is subsumed under playfulness . . .[1]

Arendt equates labour with earning a living (employment) and contrasts both with work. Perhaps she is mistaken in supposing that all people today except artists are labourers rather than workers. But the distinction she draws is an important one, and finds an echo in the remarks of one ex-miner:

. . . as I see it there are basically only two kinds of work. One is the sort that in the main is done for its own sake. Attached to it are no notions of bosses or clocks or profits or wages and usually it proves rewarding in itself. The other sort is that which is normally done in return for a weekly wage at docks, in factories, on building sites, down pits where one is a slave to timekeeping, norms, incentives, procedures . . .[2]

Definitions of Leisure

One of the chief problems of defining leisure is that it is very difficult to take an objective approach to the subject. Perhaps even more than in the case of work, the way in which someone defines leisure tends to be determined by his view of what it ought to be. There is an element of this even in the kind of definition which sees leisure as that part of time left over after work and perhaps also after other obligations have been met, because the judgment of where work leaves off and leisure begins is usually a subjective one. Between this kind of definition which concentrates on the dimension of *time*, and the openly 'normative' definition which is concerned with quality of *activity* or being, there is an approach which seeks to combine the two. We may, therefore, conveniently review various definitions of leisure which fall into these three broad groups.

What may be called the 'residual' type of definition of leisure is concerned with what is to be taken out of total time in order that leisure alone should remain. Clearly the minimum that can be taken out of all time to leave only leisure is working time in the narrow sense of employment. The author of a report on the findings of a study group on leisure exemplifies this approach:

'Leisure' was not defined in this study, save tacitly to mean the hours when a man is not working primarily for money. Those hours have to include many things; household duties, rest, relaxation, social contact, family life, voluntary work, sport and hobbies and an opportunity for a man's mind and mood and whole being to move in a different world from the world of work and production.'[3]

George Soule makes a similarly broad distinction between sold and unsold time: 'What one does in sold time is "the job" ... Time not sold, "one's own time", "free time", is thought of as leisure, no matter what one does with it.'[4]

Other residual definitions of leisure add items of varying degrees of precision to arrive at leisure time. The *Dictionary of Sociology* gives leisure as 'free time after the practical necessities of life have been attended to'[5]; and Edward Gross is equally vague in suggesting that 'leisure refers to free time, free, that is, from the need to be concerned about maintenance.'[6] George Lundberg defines leisure as 'the time we are free from the more obvious and formal duties which a paid job or other obligatory occupation imposes upon us'[7]; and, as if to apologize for the lack of objectivity in this definition as contrasted with that of work, he adds the thought that 'nearly all people can and do classify nearly all their activities according to these two categories in a way that is deeply meaningful to themselves.' Giddens is more precise about what leisure excludes, defining it 'in a residual fashion, to denote that sphere of life not occupied in working, travelling to work or sleeping,[8]' while White excludes sleeping, eating and working from the realm of leisure.[9]

The second group of definitions consists of those which start with a residual approach such as those above, but go on to include a positive description of its content or function, sometimes adding a prescriptive element. To Charles Brightbill,

leisure is time beyond that which is required for *existence*, the things which we must do, biologically, to stay alive (that is, eat, sleep, eliminate, medicate, and so on): and *subsistence*, the things we must do to make a living as in work, or prepare to make a living as in school, or pay for what we want done if we do not do it ourselves. Leisure is time in which our feelings of compulsion should be minimal. It is *discretionary* time, the time to be used according to our own judgment or choice.[10]

This is a bold attempt to satisfy criteria both of content and of quality, but it fails on at least two counts: eating and sleeping sometimes contain discretionary, as opposed to biologically necessary, elements; and subsistence tasks and the use of time according to our own judgment or choice are not necessarily mutually exclusive. Although slightly irrelevant to the problem of definition, it is worth questioning whether going to school is to prepare to make a living rather than to prepare to make a *life* (work and leisure).

Gist and Fava note the limitations of their own definition of leisure. It is

the time which an individual has free from work or other duties and which may be utilized for purposes of relaxation, diversion, social achievement, or personal development. Like many other definitions, this one does not clearly demarcate leisure from non-leisure, or leisure activity from activity that is obligatory; indeed, what is often considered leisure-time behaviour may be, in part, a response to social pressures or powerful inner drives, and may not therefore be a preferred form of behaviour.[11]

A similar approach was taken by the seminar members of the International Group of the social sciences of leisure, who drew up the following definition:

Leisure consists of a number of occupations in which the individual may indulge of his own free will – either to rest, to amuse himself, to add to his knowledge or improve his skills disinterestedly or to increase his voluntary participation in the life of the community after discharging his professional, family and social duties.[12]

The chief advantage of these two definitions over that of Brightbill is that they do not try to combine two types of criteria to distinguish leisure from non-leisure in one step, but insist that what is leisure must pass two separate tests: it must be time free from obligations (though Gist and Fava appear to raise the philosophical question of whether activities are ever really freely chosen) and it must serve specific purposes such as relaxation or community participation.

One complex definition of leisure includes not only opposition to work but a number of other criteria. Max Kaplan adopts an 'ideal type' approach which permits both subjective perception and objective analysis. His definition

contains the important elements of the situation, against which a real situation can be assessed. . . . The essential elements of leisure, as we shall interpret it, are (a) an antithesis to 'work' as an economic function, (b) a pleasant expectation and recollection, (c) a minimum of involuntary social-role obligations, (d) a psychological perception of freedom, (e) a close relation to values of the culture, (f) the inclusion of an entire range from inconsequence and insignificance to weightiness and importance, and (g) often, but not necessarily, an activity characterized by the element of play. Leisure is none of these by itself but all together in one emphasis or another.[13]

This is certainly one of the most thoughtful attempts to analyse all that is involved in leisure, but as a definition it is too broad to be useful – or to serve, in any real sense, as a definition at all. It tells us what characteristics are associated with various *functions* of leisure, rather than clearly demarcating leisure from non-leisure. The 'real situations' which are to be assessed against Kaplan's quasi-definition are presumably each man's idea of what leisure is, which is not helpful to sociological analysis.

The third group of definitions consists of those which are wholly prescriptive and normative. They stress the *quality* of leisure, though they may do this by contrasting it with the attributes of work. The various assumptions and beliefs which lie behind these definitions will be considered in more detail in the next chapter; for the present, we need only record the kinds of attributes which modern writers think leisure ought to have. The Protestant view of leisure identifies it with qualities of refinement, holding it to be unique because it is often associated with spiritual or artistic values.[14] A Catholic view as expressed by Josef Pieper is that leisure 'is a mental and spiritual attitude – it is not simply the result of external factors, it is not the inevitable result of spare time, a holiday, a week-end or a vacation It is . . . an attitude of mind, a condition of the soul, and as such utterly contrary to the ideal of "work".'[15] The disadvantage of this kind of definition from a sociological point of view is that it affords no objective criteria for making comparisons. If leisure is to be identified as an attitude of mind or a condition of soul we must ask: *which* attitude of mind and *which* condition of soul?

Unless these states of mind and soul can be expressed in terms of certain attitudes or result in certain kinds of observable behaviour, they are unlikely to get us far in the search for what distinguishes leisure from non-leisure.

When considering work, we found it necessary to distinguish the associated concepts of labour and employment. It is equally necessary to distinguish leisure from allied concepts, particularly that of free time. Although some writers (for example, Soule above) take free time to mean the same as leisure, others insist that there is a qualitative difference. Thus, according to Sebastian DeGrazia, free time is not the same as leisure.

Work is the antonym of free time. But not of leisure. Leisure and free time live in two different worlds. We have got in the habit of thinking them the same. Anybody can have free time. Free time is a realizable idea of democracy. Leisure is not fully realizable, and hence an ideal not alone an idea. Free time refers to a special way of calculating a special kind of time. Leisure refers to a state of being, a condition of man, which few desire and fewer achieve.[16]

These conceptions of 'free time' as merely time and 'leisure' as an ideal state of being may be contrasted with the views of Herbert Marcuse, who practically reverses the definitions of DeGrazia. According to Marcuse, 'the Welfare State is a state of unfreedom because its total administration is systematic restriction of (a) "technically" available free time ... (footnote: "Free time", not "leisure" time. The latter thrives in advanced industrial society, but it is unfree to the extent to which it is administered by business and politics).'[17] Both writers appear to be talking about true or 'free' leisure, but whereas DeGrazia defines it as leisure and calls into question the 'freedom' of free time, Marcuse defines it as free time and calls into question the freedom of leisure! However, leaving this largely semantic problem aside, there is a further difficulty presented by the views of DeGrazia. To say that leisure and free time live in two different worlds is another way of saying that they are not measurable by the same criteria. It is a plea against treating them as interchangeable concepts. But the distinction is not confined to the area of non-work. It applies also in the work sphere. *Some* working time is 'paid' time, but you do not have to be an employee in order to do work and in that sense 'anyone can have working time'. Yet work as a certain kind of activity, a productive relationship between man and his environment may, like leisure, be something which few desire and fewer achieve. The two worlds of time and activity are thus not the domains of work and leisure respectively, but are both *dimensions* of work *and* leisure.

Components of Life Space

'Life space' means the total of activities or ways of spending time that people have. In considering the various definitions of work and leisure we have already seen that to allocate all the parts of life space either to work or to leisure would be a gross over-simplification. It is possible to use the exhaustive categories of 'work' and 'non-work', but this still does not enable us to say where the line between the two is to be drawn. Also, important differences exist *within* as well as between these two categories. A number of writers have suggested schemes for analysing the 24 hours in the average person's day into various categories.[18] Instead of examining these schemes in detail, we may put the various categories that have been suggested into five main groups. This should make analysis easier, and it assumes that any differences among the categories in each group are fairly minor.

(1) *Work, working time, sold time, subsistence time*. Although, as we have already seen, 'work' has a wider meaning than employment, for the purpose of analysing life space it is usually identified with earning a living. If an employee is on piece rates then it is 'work', or more precisely the product of work, that he sells; if he is on time rates then he sells so much working time. However, these are both ways of measuring work *and* working time, and only differ in the way the remuneration is calculated. 'Subsistence time' lays emphasis on the *purpose* of work to the worker, that is, enabling him and his dependants to subsist.

(2) *Work-related time, work obligations*. Apart from actual working time, most people have to spend a certain amount of time in travelling to and from the place of work and in preparing or 'grooming' themselves for work. In some cases, however, at least part of the travelling time may be regarded more as a form

of leisure than as work-related – for example, time spent reading newspapers or books, chatting to fellow-travellers, or playing cards with them. Some writers regard as work-related things that would not be done if it were not for work, such as the husband doing a share of his working wife's housework. Voluntary overtime and having a second job may also be regarded as related to the main working time rather than as part of it, as may activities in the no-man's land between work and leisure such as reading on the subject of one's work when at home, attending conferences or trade union meetings which have a social as well as a work side, and so on.

(3) *Existence time, meeting physiological needs.* This is the first of three 'non-work' groups. We all have to spend a certain minimum of time on sleep and the mechanics of living – eating, washing, eliminating, etc. Beyond the minimum necessary for reasonably healthy living, extra time spent on these things may be more like a leisure activity. Eating for pleasure, taking extra care with one's appearance for a party or social occasion, sexual activity beyond the call of purely physiological need, are some examples which show that the line between the satisfaction of 'existence' needs and leisure activities is not always easy to draw.

(4) *Non-work obligations, semi-leisure.* Joffre Dumazedier, author of *Toward a Society of Leisure*, has coined the term *semi-leisure* to describe 'activities which, from the point of view of the individual, arise in the first place from leisure, but which represent in differing degrees the character of obligations.' The obligations are usually to other people, but may be to non-human objects such as pets or homes or gardens. Again, the line between obligation and leisure is not always clear and depends to a large extent on one's *attitude* to the activity. Gardening and odd-job work around the home can be a chore or an absorbing hobby, and playing with the children can be a duty or a delight.

(5) *Leisure, free time, spare time, uncommitted time, discretionary time, choosing time.* All the words after 'leisure' describe some aspect of what is meant by leisure. We saw earlier that residual

definitions of leisure give it as time free from various commitments and obligations, and that 'free' time is best regarded as a dimension of leisure. 'Spare' time is a slightly different idea, implying that, like a spare tyre, it is not normally in use but could be put to use. 'Uncommitted' time suggests lack of obligations, of either a work or non-work character. 'Discretionary' or 'choosing' time is perhaps the essence of leisure, because it means time that we can use at our own discretion and according to our own choice.

From a careful study of the various schemes for analysing life space three points emerge:

(1) Time and activity are dimensions which are *both* present in all categories of life space, even where, for the sake of brevity, both are not always stated.

(2) Between compulsory activities (in order to live or to earn a living) and freely chosen ones, some activities have the character of obligations. This applies to both work and non-work activities.

(3) Leisure implies relative freedom of choice, and it is possible to work during one's 'leisure' time.

Bearing these points in mind, a *time* scheme for the analysis of life space may be proposed:

	Work time	Non-work time		
Work	Work obligations	Physiological needs	Non-work obligations	Leisure

In this scheme work may be defined as the activity involved in earning a living, plus necessary subsidiary activities such as travelling to work. Work obligations include voluntary overtime, doing things outside normal working hours associated with the job or type of work that are not strictly necessary to a minimum acceptable level of performance in the job, or having a second job. The satisfaction of physiological needs follows the conventional definition of these needs. Non-work obligations are roughly what Dumazedier calls semi-leisure, plus the domestic work part of work obligations. Leisure is time free from obligations either to self or to others – time in which to do as one chooses.

Time and activity are *dimensions*, or ways of measuring something. The 'something' that they measure is called a *variable*. In analysing life space the crucial *time* variable seems to be whether a given space of time is work or not, while the main *activity* variable seems to be the extent to which the activity is constrained or freely chosen. The constraint may arise from within the individual himself or may be imposed on him by the way in which lives. The elements in the above time scheme may be reordered into a two-dimensional time and activity scheme:

ACTIVITY

	Constraint ←	———————————	→ *Freedom*
Work	Work (employment)	Work obligations (connected with employment)	'Leisure in work'
Non-work	Physiological needs	Non-work obligations	Leisure

(TIME)

Except for leisure, particular types of activity may be fairly easily allocated to work or non-work time. Economic necessity constrains most people to have one job (work) but only if they choose to value a higher standard of living above more free time need they take a second job (work obligation). Similarly, in the non-work sphere the satisfaction of physiological needs is in its own way as necessary as work, but non-work obligations are only obligations within a framework of prior freedom to choose; for example, a man can avoid non-work obligations connected with the conjugal family by staying single.

The position of leisure is rather special. It is clearly at the 'freedom' end of the constraint-freedom scale, but it need not be restricted to non-working time. We draw attention to this paradox when we say that someone else's way of choosing to spend leisure time looks to us more like hard work. 'Work' and 'leisure in work' may consist of the same activity; the difference is that the latter is chosen for its own sake. Thus mountaineering is work for the guide but leisure in work for the amateur climber. Leisure time and employment time cannot overlap, but there is no reason why some of the time that is sold as work should not be utilized by the seller (that is, the employee) for leisure-type activities, provided that the buyer (that is, the employer or his agent) has no objection, or is ignorant of or cannot control the situation.

In addition to such oases of leisure in the desert of working time, there remains the point that leisure means *choice*, and so time chosen to be spent as work activity – though not involving the constraint of employment – can be leisure just as much as more usual leisure activities.

Time is limited to the twenty-four hours in the day, but some human activities are such that two or more can take place at the same time. For example, the satisfaction of a physiological need, such as eating, can be accompanied by a leisure activity, such as listening to the radio. A chart of life space with only the time dimension has difficulty in coping with such simultaneous activities which fall into different categories. To overcome this difficulty the time-budget people have used the concepts of primary and secondary activities and have added the duration of the total of secondary activities to the twenty-four hours in the day to give a total daily time budget of up to thirty-two hours for some groups. As well as allocating primary and secondary activities to the same space of time, we may allocate primary and secondary functions to the same activity. Thus activities which are *primarily* at the constraint end of the scale, such as employment, may involve in a *secondary* way the leisure-like element of freely chosen activity, in this case, the type of work we should like to do even if we had no need of employment.

One important qualification must be made to the analysis of life space. In considering the various categories we have had in mind men in full-time employment. Certain modifications to the scheme are necessary if it is to fit the cases of other groups. In assuming that all adults work (i.e. are engaged in a full-time paid occupation) we should be right in about seventy per cent of cases. But an analysis of life space based on this majority would be incomplete if it could not be amended to take account of the minority who are not in a full-time occupation. We may consider the amendments to the scheme which seem to be necessary to account for the circumstances of four groups of 'non-workers': prisoners, housewives, the unemployed, and the 'idle rich'.

The life space of a prisoner is much more constricted than that of the average citizen on both time and activity dimensions. Although some prisoners are employed inside or outside the prison, the choice of available work is severely restricted and the financial motivation for it rather different (earning pocket-money rather than earning a living). In so far as some prison work may be more or less voluntarily undertaken to relieve boredom or satisfy a physiological or psychological need to work, it may resemble the 'work obligation' of ordinary citizens. But, by being cut off from the outside world, prisoners have virtually no non-work obligations, and even the character of leisure is different for them. The contrast between free and constrained activities which most of those in the outside world experience is largely denied to prisoners. The constraint to earn a living is removed, but so is the freedom to choose beyond a narrow range of institutional leisure activities, which must take place during hours set by the prison authorities. The concentration of the prisoner's activities in the middle range between economic constraint and personal freedom, and the unreality for him of the distinction between work and non-work, are measures of the narrowness of his life in prison.

It may seem strange to compare the life of the housewife to that of the prisoner, but a recent book entitled *The Captive Wife*[19] suggests that the comparison may not be entirely unwarranted. Doing the housework is, in effect, her employment but, as compared with her husband's employment, it usually offers less scope for interest and less social contact. The life of the housewife, like that of the prisoner, tends to be restricted at both ends of the constraint-freedom scale. There is for her no real difference between work and work obligations, and the responsibilities of the household, particularly if she is a mother, must often restrict the range of her leisure activities, even though her 'free time' may be greater than that of her working sister. The proportion of her time devoted to non-work obligations is correspondingly inflated. However, it is interesting to note that time budgets collected in ten countries show that non-employed women more often combine primary and secondary activities in the same space of time than do either employed men or women. In this sense at least, the lives of housewives may be fuller than those of other people.

The unemployed constitute another category whose lives show a contraction of the normal range between constraint and freedom. Many people who are unemployed develop after a time a feeling of being useless, and may be driven to occupy themselves with trivial tasks and time-filling routines. They lose the companionship and social support of workmates. Lack of money produces a restriction on the range of leisure activities which they can engage in, thus narrowing the range of life experience from the leisure and as well as the work end. But with increases in the incomes of the unemployed through such measures as wage-related unemployment benefits, people out of work may be able to purchase a 'standard of leisure' comparable to that of those in work. The position of the retired is in some ways similar to that of the unemployed, except that absence of employment is normally planned and permanent, so that in many (though by no means all) cases adjustment in the pattern of life is not too difficult to make.

In the fourth category non-workers are in a rather different position from the other three. The idle rich are free from the necessity to earn a living but this freedom, largely for reasons connected with social status, is not used to undertake work obligations. In this respect the 'work' lives of the idle rich are even more impoverished than are those of the other three categories of non-workers we have considered. But, unlike these others, the idle rich make leisure the centre of their existence. The balance of their lives is shifted heavily towards the freedom end of the scale, just as the balance of prisoners' lives is shifted towards constraint, and for both groups the distinction between work and non-work is blurred. Another minority – those who are free from the necessity of earning a living but who do work of a kind and in circumstances of their choice – are able to separate work from non-work only on the time dimension, and sometimes not even on that. They share with the idle rich a relative lack of constraint in their lives as a whole, and demonstrate 'work in leisure'. The other side of this coin – 'leisure in work' – is apparent in those people who are able to make a living in doing what they most enjoy for its own sake. Alexander Szalai hints at the possible expansion of this group when he says that 'it is by no means a natural law that productive work or work for one's living cannot offer as much inner and external freedom, as many possibilities for self-expression and relaxation, as are to be looked for and found in most cases only in leisure spent outside the working place.'[20]

In this chapter we have considered various definitions of work and leisure, and have extracted the main components of life space to throw more light on the nature of work and leisure and on other important activities and ways of spending time. We have also looked at minority groups who have different patterns of life from those of people in ordinary full-time employment. All this should help to set the scene for matters discussed in later chapters. From the statements that are made about people's work and leisure lives both now and in a possible future, it should enable us to sort out real differences and similarities.

3 Work and Leisure in History and other Societies

When discussing the problems of work and leisure we tend to take for granted the circumstances and conditions of modern industrial societies. But to understand the real range of social behaviour in these spheres we need to take a wider historical and anthropological look at work and leisure. In this chapter we shall first review the various meanings that work has had through the ages, then trace the historical development of the concept and practice of leisure, and finally compare the different ways in which work and leisure have been – and still are – related in societies other than modern industrial ones.

Historical Meanings of Work

Work, writes Marshall McLuhan in characteristically epigrammatic fashion, does not exist in a nonliterate world: it begins with the division of labour and the specialization of functions and tasks in sedentary, agricultural communities.[1] Obviously he is taking a rather narrow view of work. A more defensible statement is that work (in its widest sense, including labour) is a basic condition of the existence and continuation of human life – it is independent of any particular form of society. This does not, of course, apply to all forms of work. Only some forms are necessary to the production and reproduction of the means of life, others may be required in the development and preservation of particular types of social institution, while yet others result in the production of relatively inessential goods and services. The development of civilization corresponds in one sense to the diversity of employments in which men engage and to the expansion of the area of goods and services which are regarded as necessities. At different stages of social development, societies have various ways of defining the scope of human work in terms of the goods or services required. But there is a deeper meaning of work as itself a value that is at least partly independent of its product.

It is only for the last few decades that we have any reasonably objective documentation of the meaning of work for the mass of people. Earlier surveys, such as Henry Mayhew's classic *London Labour and the London Poor*, which covered material conditions, did not extend to attitudes to those conditions. Thus we have little or no evidence of how 'the common man' conceived of work in earlier times. The clues that we have to the various historical meanings of work must be gained from philosophical and religious writers and refer to the ideal of work held by an *élite*. For the rest, the 'problem' of the meaning of work did not exist. For most of history men have *been* what they *did*: a man's work provided him with an identity that was recognized both by others and by himself. It is also worth remembering that to ask men in economically undeveloped traditional societies why they work is similar to asking them why they try to stay alive.

To the ancient Greeks, in whose society mechanical labour was done by slaves, work was a curse and nothing else.[2] It was coloured with that sense of a heavy burdensome task which we feel in the words fatigue, travail, burden. The Greeks regarded as drudgery physical work of every sort. Work was seen as brutalizing the mind, making man unfit for thinking of truth or for practising virtue; it was a necessary material evil which the visionary *élite* should avoid. Agriculture was grudgingly accepted as not unworthy of a citizen, because it brought independence, but free artisans and craftsmen were scorned as hardly better than slaves.

Like the Greeks, the Hebrews thought of work as a painful necessity, but added the belief that it was a product of original sin. It was accepted as expiation through which man might atone for the sin of his ancestors and co-operate with God in the world's salvation. Not only intellectual but also manual work thus acquired dignity and value. Primitive Christianity followed the Jewish tradition in regarding work as punishment for original sin, but added a positive function: work is necessary above all in order to share what is produced with one's needy brothers. But no intrinsic value was recognized in labour – it was still only a means to a worthy end. Early Catholicism did something to dignify labour, but mainly of the religious and intellectual kind. Pure contemplation was placed above even intellectual monastery work. In medieval Europe heretical sects preached work not because it is good but because they believed it painful, humiliating, 'a scourge for the pride of the flesh'. As the Church drew closer to accepting worldly standards, it granted fuller justice to labour and its fruits. St Thomas Aquinas drew up a hierarchy of professions and trades, ranking agriculture first, then the handicrafts, and commerce last. But although work then appeared as a natural right and duty, it was still regarded as preferable to pray and contemplate God.

Protestantism was the force that established work in the modern mind as 'the base and key of life'. In Luther's teachings work was still natural to fallen man, but all who could work should do so. With the idea that the best way to serve God was to do most perfectly the work of one's profession, Luther swept away the distinction between religious piety and worldly activity; profession became 'calling' and work was valued as a religious path to salvation.

Calvin developed these ideas further with his concept of predestination. Only a small part of mankind shall know everlasting life; idleness and luxury are deadly sins, and dislike of work a sign that 'election' is doubtful. All men, even the rich, must work because it is the will of God. But they must not lust after the fruits of their labour. From the paradox – the command to ceaseless effort, to ceaseless renunciation of the fruits of effort – the motive power and ideological justification of modern business derives. Unlike Luther, Calvin considered it no virtue to stay in the class or profession to which one is born. It is the duty of everyone to seek out the profession which will bring him and hence society the greatest return. Work is thus freed from the hampering ideas of caste and becomes mobile and rationalized. Puritanism, developing out of Calvinism, went further yet recalled the early Christian tradition; work was valued not for love of money or pleasure but as a means whereby 'more benediction may fall upon the next needy person'. But the main legacy of Calvinism arises from its paradoxical command to deny the world but live in the world, to work hard to accumulate wealth but not to spend it on oneself. This is the foundation of the nineteenth century cult of work for the sake of work, and the abhorrence of idleness and pleasure.

However, the nineteenth century also brought a reaction to these ideas about the religious motivation of work. Since the Renaissance some men had held the view that creative work could be a joy in itself. The early Utopians had taken an essentially non-religious view of the role of work in man's life. Campanella, in his *City of the Sun* made all members of society workers who were joyful because each had work suitable to his character and which he need do for only four hours a day. In Thomas More's *Utopia* the working day is six hours, but all men take their turn at all kinds of work. The nineteenth-century socialists, contemporaries and followers of Marx and Engels, tended to be critical of the 'idealistic' implications of Utopianism, but held views on work which were broadly similar. Morelly believed that 'man is a naturally active being who does not in the least dislike work as such, but only when it is monotonous and lasts too long. If men seem to hate work that is only because arbitrary institutions have given part of mankind a perpetual holiday called prosperity, and sentenced the rest to hard labour for life.' The Marxist socialists formulated a century ago predictions which their descendants continue to hold basically today. When production is carried on solely for use and not for profit, when men are no longer compelled to work at unpleasant or boring jobs just to earn a living, they will have more zeal for work, which will be done less by routine and more by reason. It will be better organized and require less time for a greater output. Workers will have leisure time for a freer and more truly human life.

In a subsequent chapter we shall examine in greater detail the extent to which modern meanings attached to work are still influenced by some of the older conceptions. But it is worth drawing attention to another traditional way of looking at work – that common to most primitive communities still existing today. There are many parts of the world that do not have a wage system in which so much reward is given for so much labour or labour time, and in these communities it is possible to see, perhaps more clearly than in our own society, that work has functions other than economic ones. Participation in work is often undertaken as a duty towards the person who wants the work done, rather than for the material gain that can be expected from him. But work for its own sake is not regarded as a duty. This meaning of work as duty to others recalls the early Christian tradition but without its connotation as punishment for original sin.

Historical Development of Leisure

We tend to think of leisure as a product of modern civilization, and in a sense this is true. During the last hundred years we have moved from a typical 70–hour to roughly a 40–hour working week. But taking a longer historical view we see that the average man's gain in leisure with economic growth has been exaggerated. Estimates of annual and lifetime leisure suggest that the skilled urban worker may only have regained the position of his thirteenth century counterpart. This is because in medieval times about one day in three was a holiday of some kind. In the perspective of several centuries, the amount of time spent at work, at first relatively low, increased during the Industrial Revolution, and is only now decreasing to something like its earlier level.

Taking an even longer time perspective, we can see that during most of the seven or eight millennia of civilization the majority of people have had to work so hard to sustain themselves and their families that their lives have been almost devoid of leisure and spontaneous activities. The life of the peasant – and it must be remembered that the majority of mankind are still peasants – is a continuous round of labour. In the countries affected by the Hebrew tradition there is the Sabbath, but that is not so much a day of leisure as a day of ceremonial inactivity, a day of restraint. It was only at the centres where wealth accumulated or where a strong element of nomadism remained that holy days lost their severity and became holidays.

Among early civilizations the Greek and Roman cities featured leisure in something like the modern sense, though only for a privileged *élite*. To the Greeks, leisure was concerned with those activities that were worthy of a free man, activities which we might today call 'culture'. Politics, debate, philosophy, art, ritual, and athletic contests were activities worthy of a free man because they expressed the moral core of a style of life. The Greek word for leisure, *schole*, meant spare time, leisure, school. Unlike the modern conception of leisure as time saved from work, *schole* was a conscious abstention from all activities connected with merely being alive, consuming activities no less than producing. Nothing illustrates better the difference between Greek values and those of modern industrial society than their word for the work of a gentleman. They could only express it negatively as having no leisure – *ascholia*.[3]

Thorstein Veblen went back further to the barbarian stage of social development to find the origins of his 'theory of the leisure class': 'During the predatory culture labour comes to be associated in men's habits of thought with weakness and subjection to a master. It is therefore a mark of inferiority, and therefore comes to be accounted unworthy of man in his best estate. By virtue of this tradition labour is felt to be debasing, and this tradition has never died out.'[4] To gain esteem it is not sufficient merely to possess wealth or power – it must be put in evidence. This is partly achieved by conspicuous abstention from labour. The leisurely life of a ruling class is thus a means of gaining the respect of others.

In pre-industrial societies the majority of people had leisure only in the sense of mere rest from toil and of participation in stereotyped ceremonies. This was not conscious leisure, or the result of an exercise of choice, but part of the regular pattern of living. The same applied to many non-industrial societies today. In his study of the Equadorean Indians, Beate Salz notes that all their time is used, if not in work, then in other 'structured activities'.[5] Such festive occasions as weddings, christenings, birthdays and fiestas are common, and seem to have an obligatory character as well as serving as leisure activities. They are what Dumazedier calls semi-leisure and take the place of individually pursued leisure.

In the history of humanity, the idea of work in the modern sense is comparatively recent. Hans Rhee makes this point forcibly by means of a time-scale: 'if we think of humanity as having existed for one day, the notion of work as an activity in contrast to other human activities, emerged only in the last quarter of an hour.'[6] The experience of employment is, of course, an even more recent phenomenon, occupying less than a minute of humanity's day.

Work and Leisure in Non-industrial Societies

We have seen that 'work' in the early civilizations was divisible roughly according to the distinction between labour and work made by Arendt. Labour meant providing the necessities of life; it symbolized man's dependence on nature and accordingly was performed by a class of labourers or by slaves. Work, in Arendt's sense, was effort of a different kind, creative, of the spirit, performed by free men and citizens. Between work of this latter kind and leisure there could logically be no dividing line, as August Heckscher points out. 'Afterwards there was need for rest; there was need for re-creation in the exact sense of reconstituting the faculties for the pursuits of another day. But the idea that there could be a meaningful way of life, separate from the giving of themselves voluntarily to what they deemed significant and delightful, did not occur to the men of these earlier, classic periods.'[7]

Under preliterate conditions, too, the line between labour and leisure is not sharply drawn. In so far as there is no separate 'leisure class', the separation of productive activities into work and labour is also less obvious than in more civilized societies. Primitive people tend to approach a great many of their daily activities as if they were play. The orientation of life is towards long periods of work interspersed with occasional periods of intense expenditure of energy. Rosalie Wax remarks on this fusion of work and leisure: 'I do not believe that any Bushman could tell us – or would be interested in telling us – which part of [his] activity was work and which was play.'[8] Life in primitive societies follows a predetermined pattern in which work and non-work are inextricably confused. In these societies there are no clearly defined periods of leisure as such, but economic activities, like hunting or market-going, obviously have their recreational aspects, as do singing and telling stories at work. Though there are things done for enjoyment and recreation, the idea of time being set aside for this purpose is unfamiliar.

Work in co-operation is a frequent aspect of primitive economic life. The stimulus given by work in company with songs and jokes lightens drudgery and gives it some tinge of recreation. H. Ashton describes the co-operative work-parties (*matsema*) which are a feature of all phases of agricultural work among the Basuto: 'These are gay, sociable affairs comprising about 10–50 participants of both sexes ... These *matsema* are useful though not very efficient. They assemble in the morning about 9 o'clock and work, with frequent breaks for light refreshment, until about 3 or 4 o'clock in the afternoon, to the accompaniment of ceaseless chatter and singing.'[9] If labour is seen merely as a factor in production then this kind of behaviour is 'inefficient'. But the point is that it is useful to the people involved, that is, it is a preferred pattern. Work has its own psychological gains and losses, and it is no simple matter to decide the ways in which these balance up to provide a resultant of satisfaction or deprivation.

However, some pre-industrial societies do make a distinction between work and leisure, in a way that is quite close to the contemporary, although not to the traditional, Western pattern. Thus the lives of the Baluchi of Western Pakistan are divided into a sphere of duty or obligation necessary for life in civil society and an area which they call the sphere of one's own will.[10] They seem to regard the latter as being a sphere of freedom and distraction from the workaday world. But whereas the Western tradition is to see the workaday world as the foundation of existence, the Baluchi invert the emphasis. For them – as indeed for growing numbers of people in Western society today – the world of their own will is the cherished area, the one in which they spend their energy and imagination and ingenuity.

At one point in its history one relatively sophisticated culture made so sharp a distinction between work and sacred activities that a combination of the two was viewed as blasphemous.[11] This was the rigorously enforced leisure of the pious medieval Jew who, when engaged in sacred matters, avoided anything remotely connected with work. But though it was the polar opposite of practical mundane activity, Judaic piety was by no means the same as play or free time. Indeed, it entailed more work and more trouble than any of the stringent, time-consuming activities of the secular world.

One of the biggest differences in the meaning of leisure is that between urban and rural communities. Leisure in agricultural societies is structured by the rhythm of necessary daily tasks and of the seasons, and is embedded in life rather than a separate part of it. This is the case in traditional Japanese society in which any leisure consciously conceived as such is seasonal rather than daily, weekly or monthly. The point is also illustrated by the reaction of Texan homesteaders to the possibility of inheriting a large fortune. Some thought they would take time off to go hunting and fishing but no one considered complete leisure a possible way of life.[12]

What are the general conclusions to be drawn from studies of work and leisure in types of society other than our own? First, work seems usually to have been identified with the constraint of labour, though the forms that this constraint has taken – as an obstacle to 'higher things', as a purgative, or as social duty – are today absent or muted themes when compared with the economic constraint to earn a living. Secondly, sandwiched between the earlier religious views of work and the nineteenth century Protestant cult of work for the sake of work, there was the Renaissance view of work as creative, intrinsically satisfying activity. Thirdly, the absence of a sharp demarcation between work and leisure in most preliterate and rural societies has two aspects: the more leisurely character of work, but the greater importance of non-work obligations as compared with the type of leisure most often experienced in modern industrial societies. And lastly, the degree to which work and leisure are experienced in fact and in ideology as separate parts of life seems to be related to the degree to which the society itself is stratified, work being the lot of the masses and leisure of the *élite*.

What do these conclusions imply for the future of work and leisure in our own society? If automation and other technological advances will mean that a smaller proportion of our time (or the time of a smaller proportion of people) must be devoted to earning a living, it is quite possible that some of the older meanings of work will reassert themselves. For most people leisure is now definitely marked off from work, but historically this may be seen as a pleasure-seeking reaction to a philosophy of work for the sake of work. There is no reason to suppose that this reaction will go on for ever. Perhaps the biggest question mark hangs over the future of the class system. Hitherto there have been 'working classes' and 'leisure classes' (i.e. privileged classes of one kind or another). Today, although the social system is still based on private property with consequent inequality and privilege, there are working people who are also people of leisure – mass leisure. So those who believe in *élites* may have to pin their faith to differences in the *style* of both work and leisure rather than to the exclusive class participation in one *or* the other. On the other hand, those who favour social equality will seek to make work a more rewarding experience for the mass of people and to narrow the gap between the 'highbrow' and 'lowbrow' kinds of leisure.

4 The Experience and Meaning of Work Today

In this chapter we shall look at the different ways in which men and women earn their living in our society and the different meanings that work has for them. The various sources of satisfaction and dissatisfaction that people have in their work tell us something about how well or how badly the content and organization of the work is suited to their needs. The different meanings that people tend to attach to work according to the type of job they do, and the widespred feeling of alienation from work, are other aspects that merit attention. Finally we may consider the probable changes in the occupational structure that are likely to affect satisfaction, meaning and alienation from work.

The statements that follow are based on data from two sources: (1) surveys carried out by various social researchers, including myself,[1] and (2) case studies from *New Left Review*'s two volumes of *Work: Twenty Personal Accounts*.[2] It is hoped that this mixture of the statistically respectable with the humanly interesting will be more acceptable than either source alone.

Work Satisfaction

Many occupations have been the subject of work satisfaction studies, though factory and office work have predominated. Among skilled factory workers and craftsmen intrinsic satisfaction with the work itself is frequently found, especially when the job involves the completion of a whole product. Assembly-line workers attach more importance to being able to control to some extent the pace and methods of their work. Variety of operations is a source of satisfaction to both factory and office workers, and among the latter the friendliness of the working group is often mentioned (particularly by women). In comparing proportions of satisfied workers in different occupations, there seem to be separate scales for manual and non-manual jobs, with more satisfaction found at the higher levels of skill in each group.

43

Professional workers are most satisfied, and semi-skilled and unskilled manual workers least so.

Of 'special situation' factors which influence satisfaction, social interaction seems to be most important. Insecurity in a job, even when accompanied by good objective conditions, adversely affects satisfaction. Autonomy in the work situation – freedom to make decisions and take responsibilities – is positively related to satisfaction. If three individuals are engaged on the same work with mates doing respectively a better, worse, or the same job, the first is likely to show least job enjoyment. Permissive supervision and leadership, and being consulted in advance about changes in work processes, are conducive to satisfaction. In general, jobs which involve dealing with people provide more satisfaction than those which do not.

The above is a brief summary of some of the main findings from surveys of work satisfaction. These findings give us some idea of the sources of satisfaction and the features of jobs which produce satisfaction, but we need the benefit of more personal accounts to understand the full richness – and also the relative poverty – of people's working lives. If we put these personal accounts within a framework then we can preserve both a personal approach and a systematic one: we understand *people* more fully and we understand *society* more fully.

Let us first consider some of the main themes which emerge from people's statements about what makes work satisfying to them:

(1) *Creating something*. This is compounded of a feeling that one has put something of oneself into a product and a deep sense of pleasure in the act of creation itself. It is perhaps the most common of all the expressed feelings of satisfaction and felt by the widest range of workers, both manual and non-manual. Referring to steelmaking in the early years of the present century, a steelman writes that 'every pot of steel was an act of creation. It was something derived from the absorbed attention of dedicated men.' An accountant describes his work partly as 'an act of creation, i.e. if the thing is right there is a form about it, a kind of beauty which comes from its structure; it exists that way because it has been made from the right bits and pieces.'

Sometimes the feeling of creating something is linked to how the thing created fits into the scheme of things. Thus toolmaking 'was obviously a source of much ego-contentment and status. Each man made a complete tool, jig or punch and die by himself.' Even a product which is in fact created by a number of people can give satisfaction to the one who can feel that it is really 'his'. A journalist, otherwise indifferent to his work, writes that 'for the time it took me to re-read one of "my" stories in the papers next day, I too felt the satisfaction of having created.'

(2) *Using skill.* This is often associated with creating something, but it lays more emphasis on what the work does for the person rather than the product. Again, the use of skill cuts across the manual-nonmanual division of work. 'The skilled worker has to work out, from drawings, the best method of doing the particular job; he has to set his own machine, he has to get the necessary tools out of the stores, he has to grind his own tools and so on. Using his ingenuity and his skill, the worker is constantly made aware of his active and valuable role in the productive process.' The bricklayer finding 'a certain joy in being able to do something competently with one's hands and in using muscular force with common sense to overcome obstacles', and the computer programmer delighting in the scope his job has for technical ingenuity are other examples of the different ways in which satisfaction can be gained from the use of skills.

(3) *Working wholeheartedly.* Various restrictions on full productive effort by workers (attempting to beat the rate-fixer or time-study man, working to rule, 'go-slows' etc.), are common in industry today. But there is no evidence that these are *preferred* patterns of working and they mostly exist as weapons in the battle to get more money. More enlightened management policies than most existing ones could surely turn to better account the knowledge that most people enjoy working wholeheartedly provided that they do not feel that they lose financially by doing so. A salesman expresses this idea clearly and simply: 'Like most people, I enjoy working wholeheartedly when I work.' A bricklayer says that 'the jobs I have enjoyed most are those where I have worked the hardest.' A slight variation of this theme is the fact that few people like to turn out sub-standard work.

(4) *Using initiative and having responsibility*. This theme includes a feeling of freedom to take decisions and a certain independence of authority in the sense of people telling you what to do. To some extent the satisfaction derived from a job having these characteristics is a matter of personality and upbringing. Someone who has been raised and educated in the tradition of conformity and subservience to authority may not wish to use his initiative or have responsibility in his job. But it seems that most people value the opportunity to think and act in their work as responsible and relatively autonomous individuals. Even those workers who are 'not paid to think' often find it helps the job to go well if they do. A machine minder will replace the broken part of a machine without calling the supervisor because 'it's quicker and more interesting to do it yourself.' Another aspect of responsibility is well expressed by the doctor's secretary who found that 'one of the chief attractions of the job for me is the feeling of being in charge, feeling that I matter. . . . I would certainly be missed if I left.'

(5) *Mixing with people*. This is an outstanding source of satisfaction to people whose work involves dealing with customers or clients.[3] The attraction may lie in the variety of people one meets, the feeling of being able to help or teach others, the use of independent judgment as in casework, or simply the pleasure derived from social contact. A teacher writes that his job is 'concerned with growing and developing individuals who are never predictable, and so provide a variety of experience which is always stimulating.' Those whose work brings them into regular contact with other people may not always feel (as does one minister) 'increasingly refreshed and healed by personal encounter', but at least they will mostly agree with the doctor's secretary that 'it is much more interesting to follow cases then costs.'

(6) *Working with people who know their job*. The 'human relations' school of industrial sociology stresses how important it is to have good communication between managers and workers and that it helps if managers show a friendly and interested approach towards their workers. However, if this is merely used as a

technique, people tend to 'see through it'. A deeper respect seems to be accorded bosses who really know their job. Among the things that one town planner looks for in a job is the opportunity 'to work for people who know how to get a job done and who are not afraid or ashamed to be seen to be responsible'. Mutual respect is looked for; in the words of a steelman, 'to know that a manager knew his job and that he respected one reciprocally was a good thing all round, good for the metal, good for the melter, and good for the manager'.

So far we have described some of the positive satisfactions that people gain from their work. What can be said of the things that cause dissatisfaction? Obviously some of these are simply the opposite of the things discussed above – not being able to create anything using no skill, and so on. But the emphases are rather different. Again, drawing on a number of *New Left Review*'s accounts, we can see several themes of dissatisfaction:

(1) *Doing repetitive work.* This produces a feeling of never really achieving anything and of failing to use one's human faculties. It has long been recognized as a problem in industry and attempts to ameliorate it include shifting workers from one job to another as frequently as possible (job rotation). The full effect of repetitive work on human beings is incalculable, but we have the evidence of a few articulate victims. 'Nothing is gained from the work itself – it has nothing to offer. . . . Either one job is followed by another which is equally boring, or the same job goes on for ever: particles of production that stretch into an age of inconsequence. There is never a sense of fulfilment.' Sometimes fully mechanical work may be preferred to work which requires a little attention because it enables the person to absent himself mentally from the job. Thus a housewife complains of 'the sameness of jobs that require perhaps less than a quarter of one's mental awareness, while leaving the rest incapable of being occupied elsewhere.'

(2) *Making only a small part of something.* Long ago Karl Marx drew attention to what he called the excessive division of labour under capitalism: the forcing of men into a specialization of function that becomes more and more narrow and less and less

inclusive of their various potentials of ability. Despite some attempts to give people more of a whole job to do (job enlargement) there is still plenty of work that in effect makes the worker, in Marx's phrase, an appendage to a machine. One operative expresses the view that 'the worker's role is becoming more and more that of an onlooker and less that of a participant. . . . The loss of dignity and restriction of talent compatible with modern factory life cause a lack of quality in the factory worker.' To a toolmaker, 'the normal lot of the industrial worker is a very unsatisfactory work experience of performing a fragmented task under conditions he can only marginally control.' These observations suggest that fragmented tasks not only mean less participation by the worker in the total work process but also affect his whole way of life and restrict his personal development.

(3) *Doing useless tasks*. It can be argued that any work for which someone is prepared to pay or to authorize payment presumably has a use. But this ignores the extent to which the whole system of production and distribution has become remote from direct personal needs as it has become 'mass'. Much of the growth in the service occupations has to do with protecting property. A nightwatchman describes his work group as 'a hive of men guarding the sleep of capital. Producing nothing, this labour exists to make nothing happen, its aim is emptiness.' Another type of task commonly felt to be useless is form-filling. In offices, factories, schools and hospitals the amount of paperwork is steadily increasing. The occupations it provides are seldom satisfying to the people concerned. Writing about himself and his fellows, a clerk remarks that 'unlike even the humblest worker on a production line, he doesn't produce *anything*. He battles with phantoms, abstracts: runs in a paper chase that goes on year after year, and seems utterly pointless.'

(4) *Feeling a sense of insecurity*. The recurrent economic difficulties of the country, combined with technological and organizational changes, have resulted in an increase in the number of workers being made redundant. This, in turn, has led to mounting fears about the security of jobs. As previously noted, a feeling of insecurity seems to spill over into dissatisfaction with many

other aspects of a job. Few people seem able to analyse their feelings of insecurity but many of them mention it in talking about their work. 'There is a general feeling of frustration, a feeling that life has little purpose in such insecure conditions where everyone is threatened with the loss of his job.' (Warehouseman). Sometimes the loss of a job is at least partly looked forward to. 'You feel dispensable, interim: automation will take [the job] over one day, the sooner the better.' (Clerk).

(5) *Being too closely supervised.* Much has been learned by industrial researchers about the most appropriate and acceptable forms of supervision, but few of the lessons seem to have been learned by management. Office workers are more often the victims of inhuman supervisory systems than are factory workers. The clerk quoted above describes the worst kind, 'those that have you lined up in rows facing the front, with the eagle eye on you and no excuse for moving at all'. In social work and teaching the grievances concerning supervision take a rather different form. A child care officer explains how the 'hierarchy' is a drag on growth and change: 'What each of us needed in the job was the awareness to know what people were really saying, or trying to say, and to then decide how we could help them. To be assigned a role in a hierarchy contributed nothing to that.' Similarly a teacher complains that the bureaucratic structure of the school means that the school governors and senior staff 'wish to supervise the minutest details of the projects they organize'.

The themes of satisfaction and dissatisfaction discussed above cover many aspects of the jobs that most people do today. Much more could be said, and the interested reader may wish to follow up the subject in the books and journals which deal with work satisfaction surveys.[4] Perhaps the most remarkable thing about the findings in general is the large gap they show between the most rewarding and the least rewarding kinds and conditions of work – a gap that cannot be entirely justified by the differences in the actual and potential abilities of the people concerned.

Meanings of Work

The concept of 'meaning' overlaps that of satisfaction (or dissatisfaction). When someone says that he finds his work satisfying because it is, for example, creative this is a way of saying that the work has meaning for him, that he can see the purpose for which it is done and that he agrees with this purpose. On the other hand, a worker may be dissatisfied with his job because he feels it to be 'meaningless' in the sense of not understanding where his contribution fits into the whole, or even (in the case of highly fragmented work) not knowing what that contribution is. Strictly speaking, of course, any kind of work must mean *something*, even if it is nothing more than a way of earning a living.

A number of studies have sought to define various meanings of work held by people in different occupations and work situations. Weiss and Kahn found that over three-fourths of respondents defined work either as activity which was necessary though not enjoyed or as activity which was scheduled or paid for.[5] The first definition was associated with occupations which permit some autonomy (professionals and salespeople), and the second with occupations with neither social standing nor autonomy (factory workers and labourers). Friedmann and Havighurst compared the meaning of work to five occupational groups.[6] The workers of lower skill and socioeconomic status were more likely to see their work as having no other meaning than that of earning money. Coal-miners had a more personal sense than steel-workers of being pitted against their environment and expressed feelings of accomplishment and pride at having conquered it. Skilled craftsmen showed a very high degree of emphasis on work as a source of self-respect and the respect of others. All of the salespeople surveyed recognized some meaning in their work beyond earning a living, and the most popular meanings were 'something to do and think about' and sociability and friendship. Finally, the physicians were found to stress most the public service aspect of their jobs.

The method used by Morse and Weiss to study the meaning of work was to ask people whether they would continue working if they inherited enough money to live comfortably without working.[7] They concluded that to those in middle-class occupations work means having something interesting to do, having a chance to accomplish things, and to contribute, while those in working-class occupations view work as synonymous with activity. These differences in work meanings correspond to differences in the content of the jobs. The content of professional, managerial and sales jobs concerns symbols and the handling of cases, and so a life without such work would be less purposeful, stimulating and challenging. Working-class occupations emphasize working with tools and machines, and the individual is oriented to the effort rather than to the end-product – life without such work would mean life without anything to do.

A threefold division of the meaning of work less fragmented than that of Friedmann and Havighurst but less oversimplified than that of Morse and Weiss is suggested by Peter Berger:

First, there is work that still provides an occasion for primary self-identification and self-commitment of the individual – for his 'fulfilment', if one prefers. *Thirdly*, there is work that is apprehended as a direct threat to self-identification, an indignity, an oppression. And secondly, between these two poles, is work that is *neither* fulfilment nor oppression, a sort of gray, neutral region in which one neither rejoices nor suffers, but with which one puts up with more or less grace for the sake of other things that are supposed to be important. ... In the first category, of course, are to be placed most so-called professions and the upper-echelon positions in the various bureaucratic apparatuses. In the third category continue to remain many of the unskilled occupations 'in the basement' of the industrial system. And in between, in the second category, is to be found the bulk of both white-collar and blue-collar work.[8]

The findings of these studies have had to be compressed here, but they can be seen to fit in with many of the personal accounts quoted in the previous section. The conclusions of the studies have been couched in the language used by the researchers themselves, and reveal a certain amount of middle-class bias. Undoubtedly there *are* broad differences in the meanings attached to work, but we must beware of too-sweeping generalizations. Not all middle-class and professional occupations are 'fulfilling' to their holders although a desire to achieve status or success may lead to exaggerated claims about the most trivial and socially useless occupations. On the other hand, the poor economic and social rewards of many so-called working-class occupations should not obscure their real value both to society and (less often) to the workers themselves.

The meaning of work varies with three factors: type of occupation (skills used), industry (use to which the skills are put), and status (position in the employing organization or in society). In many cases the content of the work will vary with employment status, but even where the content of the work is the same or very similar work attitudes may vary according to status. Thus laboratory workers were found to differ in their work values according to whether they were 'professionals' or 'technicians' even though both groups had roughly the same kind of tasks.[9] The professionals were far more likely to say that the kind of work they did was the most important thing about a life's work, while the technicians more often said that security or pay was the most important thing.

A notable difference in status, or *social* position in society, is perhaps better understood as a difference in class, or *economic* position in society: that between workers and capitalists. The term 'capitalist' has pejorative overtones, but as applied to those persons who possess capital the return on which enables them to live without the necessity of being employed it has a reasonably precise meaning. The term 'employer' can in fact be a misleading antonym of 'employee' if it denotes a person who hires and fires employees, since that person, no less than those he hires and fires, may himself be an employee of an organization owned by shareholders or controlled by the state or other public authority. There is nothing to stop a capitalist being an employee, though naturally he will usually choose to be an employee at a high status level appropriate to his economic position.

Those highly paid employees at managerial level who approach the economic position of capitalists are able, because of their stronger bargaining position, to obtain favourable terms of employment, often including the ability to determine their own working hours. Their work, though more demanding, is usually intrinsically more interesting, partly because they make decisions instead of having to conform to other people's decisions. In short, we may divide people into three broad groups with regard to work experience: the capitalists, who have no need of employment but may work if they wish (minimum constraint); the managers, who are employed on favourable terms (medium constraint); and the mass of employees, who are compelled to work for a living (maximum constraint). Inevitably, work must mean different things to these three groups.

Alienation from Work

The theme of alienation from work is widely used to describe the disengagement of self from the occupational role. As some of the personal accounts showed, workers tend to become frustrated by the lack of meaning in the tasks allotted to them and by the impersonality of their role in the work organization. Such workers are virtually forced to turn to non-work life for a sense of values and identity: 'I only work here, but if you want to know me as I really am, come to my home and meet my family.'[10] Alienation can also take subtler forms among professionals and executives, for whom it may be fashionable to be cynical about one's work but quite 'satisfied' with one's job. Experience of alienation is not confined to a few special occupations, though it tends to be associated with certain characteristic work situations. In bureaucratic organizations it is apparent in the administration of men as if they were things. In an automated factory or office it takes the form of increasing the number of people who deal with the world through abstractions.

An important contribution to understanding the nature and correlates of alienation from work has been made by Robert Blauner.[11] In making a comparative analysis of four types of work situation he demonstrates convincingly that alienation is a function of the type of industry in which people work. He analysed the dimensions of alienation as *powerlessness* (inability to control the work process), *meaninglessness* (inability to develop a sense of purpose connecting the job to the overall productive process), *isolation* (inability to belong to integrated industrial communities), and *self-estrangement* (failure to become involved in the activity of work as a mode of self-expression). The four types of industry compared were printing, textiles, automobile and chemical. The general picture was of a relative lack of alienation in craft printing, an increase in machine textiles, a further increase in the assembly-line automobile industry, but a reduction to something like the printing level in the automated chemical industry.

The Changing Occupational Structure

Until the middle of the eighteenth century the British were predominantly an agriculturally employed population. Since then there has been a steady drift from the land and this is likely to continue. Farm workers have low incomes and therefore few leisure pursuits that cost money, but they usually like their work. They favourably compare its variety and its creativity with monotonous and fragmented factory work, which they sometimes try and then give up. Mining is another diminishing occupational category and, because of its effect on health, miners are more likely to welcome than to regret a change of work.

In industry generally there has been a levelling of the use of skill and this, too, is likely to continue. Both craftsmen and unskilled manual workers are steadily being replaced by operatives in semi-automated plants. It is claimed that as we move towards full automation work will become 'humanized' – the machines will do all the hard and routine work, leaving man free to plan and control. The difference between semi-automation and full automation may, from the worker's point of view, represent an increase in the meaning of work. To that extent, automation is to be encouraged for what it can do for people as well as production. But not all the production of goods and services is going to be automated, and the aim of making the experience of work more meaningful stands in its own right.

With the continuing growth in the social and welfare services there will be increasing numbers of jobs involving dealing with people, many of which jobs will be regarded as more rewarding than most of those which are declining in numbers. The implication of the growth in the 'leisure industries' for the meaning of work is not so clear. Unless there is a move away from commercialized amusement and towards do-it-yourself leisure pursuits, more people are likely to spend their working lives ministering to the leisure needs of others. At this stage we can only speculate on the effect that these changes will have on the meaning of work; more definite knowledge depends on the product of another growth industry: that of social research.

5 Kinds of Leisure and their Meaning Today

This is the age of increasing leisure, we are constantly told. But what *kind* of leisure? There are many ways of filling free time, ways which amount to a complex 'machinery of amusement', all the parts of which *look* different while probably performing in many cases the same function to the individual. And what of society itself – does it have an interest in the enjoyment of its leisure-seekers in any way comparable to its interest in the productivity of its workers? In a parallel exercise to that undertaken in the previous chapter we may look at the research findings on both the use of leisure time and the meaning attached to leisure.

Social and Individual Functions of Leisure

Leisure has functions in the life of an individual, and its experience by individuals and groups has functions for the society in which they live. We may consider first how leisure serves society. It does this in three main ways: it helps people to learn how to play their part in society; it helps them to achieve societal or collective aims; and it helps the society to keep together.[1] These functions apply to groups as well as to the wider society.

The word sociologists have for describing the process by which people learn how to play their part in society is 'socialization'. It starts in childhood but continues into adult life as people have to learn how to cope with new situations and to fit in – more or less – with what is expected of them. Leisure in the form of play and story-telling is used as a technique for teaching young children and reconciling them to school work. Leisure in the form of horseplay and initiation ceremonies often helps to socialize young workers into their jobs.

The work essential to society is aided by the recreational function of leisure. After a certain point work results in fatigue and often in boredom. With the intention of increasing productivity, some firms allow their workers more breaks than are strictly necessary for physiological purposes. Other firms encourage their workers to take 'wholesome recreation' off the job (the whole subject of industrial recreation will be dealt with in the next chapter). In another sense, industry needs the consuming time of workers as much as it needs their producing time. Businessmen in the 'leisure industries' are interested in making leisure serve economic purposes by encouraging people to buy leisure goods and to pay for leisure services. But a trade unionist, Mr E. S. Williams, made the following remarks in seconding a motion on reduced working hours and increased holidays:

I would draw attention of the Congress to the need for our Movement to intensify its efforts among workpeople to ensure their full understanding of the need for adequate rest and leisure periods as essentials in the modern world of speed, speed and more speed. Intensification of effort over shorter working periods must be accompanied not only by longer rest and leisure periods but also by a full appreciation among our people of the need for them to use such leisure time in the pursuit of relaxation of their physical and mental processes which are of such importance in the modern industrial world.[2]

It is not suggested that the views of Mr Williams are typical of trade unionists – his subordination of leisure to the needs of industry is more typical of the nineteenth-century cult of work than of the twentieth century cult of leisure. But old ideas die hard. Also under the heading of societal aims there is the motivation that leisure may provide for work. Acquiring expensive leisure objects such as boats or caravans may only be possible through extra work (in the form either of overtime or a second job), and the prospects of a life of total leisure may be the motive for certain types of gambling, such as the big football pools.

Finally, leisure may contribute to the integration of society by promoting solidarity. At work, people may behave in leisure-like ways, such as 'horsing around', which help them to feel a sense of belonging together. Play and sporting activities serve as focal points of group identification. This raises the question of the degree of organization that is permissible in leisure activities.

There is a paradox in planning for the use of what is supposed to be an uncommitted part of one's life. Since, however, the provision of leisure opportunities and the spread of ideas about how leisure time should be spent are largely functions of society, there is no guarantee that the absence of planning would increase the individual's choice of leisure opportunities. We shall return to this subject in the final chapter.

The state's attitude to the use of leisure by its citizens reflects both its function as an integrative institution and the shared values of those it controls. All states in the modern industrial world need to exercise at least a minimal control over the leisure activities of individuals. Some types of leisure behaviour or the provision of leisure facilities are defined as illegal, and the 'leisure industries' are subject to the same general laws which control other enterprises. Beyond this, the attitude of the state to the use of leisure may vary both with its degree of economic development and with the political views of the electorate. Countries such as China, having only recently embarked on the road to industrialization, require their citizens to render additional service to the state in their free time, to engage in organized physical culture for greater work efficiency, and to use entertainment, music, literature and art to reinforce the state's economic objectives. Russia, becoming like America in many economic if not social respects, dilutes a utilitarian approach to leisure with a liberal dose of concern for the development of the individual: 'Two major themes permeate the official discussion of leisure. One is the interdependence of leisure and work, that is, the contribution which well-spent leisure can make to efficiency at work; the other is the relationship between leisure and the "all-round development of the personality".'[3] In America and Britain government as such tends not to attempt to influence leisure activities, although the big business of commercialized leisure imposes its own standards of conformity.

Turning now to the functions of leisure for the individual, these can be classified on the basis of observed behaviour. An important classification is that of Dumazedier, who believes that leisure has three main functions of relaxation, entertainment, and personal development.[4] Relaxation provides recovery from fatigue, and repairs the physical and nervous damage wrought by the tensions of daily pressures, and particularly by those of the job. Entertainment provides relief from boredom – a break from daily routine. It has a strong element of escape – *realistic* in the form of a change of place or style (trips, sports), and involving *fantasy* in the form of identification and projection (cinema, the novel, etc.). In their extreme form these active and passive entertainment functions of leisure may be compared respectively with the 'compensatory' and 'spillover' hypotheses of Harold Wilensky, the former involving 'explosive compensation for the deadening rhythms of factory life' and the latter referring to the situation where mental stultification produced by work permeates leisure.[5]

Dumazedier's third function of leisure – personal development – 'serves to liberate the individual from the daily automatism of thought and action. It permits a broader, readier social participation on the one hand, and on the other, a willing cultivation of the physical and mental self over and above utilitarian considerations of job or practical advancement. It may even lead to discovering new forms of voluntary learning for the rest of one's life and induce an entirely new kind of creative attitude'. Dumazedier observes that the three functions are interdependent and exist in varying degrees in everyone's life. They may coexist in a single leisure situation or may be exercised in turn.

Less comprehensive assessments of the roles of leisure may be fitted into the Dumazedier classification. One example is William Faunce's statement that 'leisure may be recuperative in the sense that time is spent relaxing from the job completed and preparing for the job forthcoming or it may be actively spent in the sense of physical or emotional involvement in an activity. . . . Leisure time may serve as a relief from boredom or as an escape from involvement.'[6] A. Giddens's remarks on the two major psychological functions of play noted are slightly different ways of talking about relaxation and personal development: cathartic (dissipating tension accumulated in other spheres) and ego-expansion (satisfactions of achievement and self-realization which are frustrated elsewhere).[7]

The type of work experience does not enable us to predict actual leisure behaviour, but it does enable us to predict what sort of function may be served for the individual by leisure behaviour. Those who want excitement, as well as those who want quiet, may only be searching for compensations for the kind of working life they have. For example, excitement may be sought in leisure because most of one's working life is dull; and the duller it is, the cruder the excitement that is satisfying. In the preface to a study of pigeon cultivation among French miners, Georges Friedmann pointed out that leisure does more than merely offer a compensation for the technique of work. It brings professional compensations for work with a limited horizon, emotional compensations for the crudity of social relations in a mass of people, and social compensations through the success which this leisure-time activity can provide. After quoting this study, Dumazedier and Latouche observe that, far from being a compensation, leisure is more often only an extension of occupational life.[8] They refer to a study by Louchet showing that there is a tendency for the most frustrating leisure to be associated with the most frustrating work.

The Use of Leisure by Occupational Groups

How much leisure time people have and the ways in which they use it depend to a large extent on how much of their time and energies they invest in their jobs. Few studies have been made of the duration of leisure time for various occupational groups, no doubt partly because of the difficulty of defining leisure time. In the American suburban study by Lundberg and his associates in the early 1930s the average leisure time of male white-collar workers was reported as 438 minutes per day and that of executives as 401 minutes, but this included eating time.[9] Without giving figures, Harold Wilensky deduces from the comparative lengths of work weeks and work obligations that professionals, executives, officials and proprietors have less leisure time than the 'masses'.[10] In Poland the daily estimated time spent as leisure was 3.5 hours for workers in manufacturing industries, 2 hours for railwaymen, 3 hours for clerks, teachers and engineers and 2 hours for scientists and physicians.[11] It was noted that railwaymen read newspapers and even books during their working time, so their total time for leisure activities probably does not constitute an exception to Wilensky's broad generalisation.

Many more studies have been made of *types* of leisure behaviour in different occupational groups. The first national recreation survey in Britain showed that 'the higher the income level, occupational class and educational status of contacts, the greater the number of pursuits they mentioned for their weekend before interview, and the greater the importance of the "active" compared with the "passive" recreations. In short, those with the highest socio-economic status not only do more things, but do more active things. . . .'[12] A Government Social Survey report gave similar findings: employers, managers and professional people watched only half as much television, but participated nearly twice as often in physical recreation, as semi-skilled and unskilled manual workers.[13] The *choice* of recreation also varies among occupational groups. Among employers and managers eighteen per cent play golf, compared with less than five per cent in the manual groups. Soccer is predominantly the game of manual workers, while cricket is more popular among the non-manual. Income is not a factor in this last choice, because participation in the two games costs about the same. Soccer is on the whole a rougher and tougher game than cricket and may fit in better with a manual worker's idea of what is a manly sport. It is also a sport requiring closer co-operation between members of a team, reflecting more the content of working-class occupations than of individualistic middle-class occupations.

Various American studies confirm the conclusion that occupation is related to certain preferred ways of spending leisure. For example, Joel Gerstl found that college professors spent less time with their children and around the home and less time on sport and non-professional organizations than did either admen or dentists.[14] Instead the professors tended to have 'work in leisure' by reading around their subject. Saxon Graham concluded that the proportion of professional workers participating in strenuous exercise was nearly twice that of unskilled workers.[15]

Other studies have been made in terms of wider class or status groups, which may reveal some occupational differences while obscuring others. According to R. Clyde White, the upper middle class more often use libraries and have home diversions and lecture-study groups, while the two lowest classes more often use parks and playgrounds, 'community chest' organizations, churches, museums and community entertainment.[16] Leonard Reissman found that those in higher class positions were more active and diverse in their social participation than those in lower classes and that the middle class tended to dominate the organizational activity of the community.[17] Alfred Clarke concluded that 'spectatoritis' occurred most often at the middle level of occupational prestige and that craft interest tended to vary inversely with prestige level.[18]

A study has been made of the leisure activities of a group of workers on rotating shifts, whose hours of work fall at all times of the day or night, during the week and at week-ends.[19] As compared with day workers, the rotating shift workers in this sample tended to belong to fewer organizations and to go to meetings less often, and had fewer activities in which participation can occur only at specific times. Activities, like visiting, that can occur at different times were less affected, and those that can occur at any time, like indoor work and hobbies, were increased.

The Meaning of Leisure

'The meaning of leisure in a given civilization depends on the meaning given to work. ... What the individual demands of leisure depends on what he has and has not found in his work, and on what the education he has received has made him.'[20] These propositions by Raymond Aron are consistent with such impressions and evidence as we have but they can scarcely be said to have been adequately researched.

Most of the reported research on subjective meanings of leisure has been carried out by Robert Havighurst and his associates. They did not use type of occupation as a specific variable, but some clues to the meaning of leisure for occupational groups can be gained from the analysis of social class groups. In a study of the leisure activities of a sample of middle-aged people in Kansas City, Havighurst concluded that different age, sex and social class groups can derive similar values from their leisure, even though its content is different.[21] A comparative study was carried out in New Zealand, and leisure was found to have about the same meaning in the two countries. The principal meanings (defined as felt satisfactions or reasons for carrying on a particular leisure activity) in order of frequency were: just for the pleasure of doing it, a welcome change from work, brings contact with friends, gives new experience, makes the time pass, and gives the feeling of being creative.[22] Certain differences according to sex and social class were found: for example, the 'creative' meaning was more often expressed by women, and working-class people tended to stress the 'makes time pass' meaning.[23]

Havighurst agrees with Aron that most of the meanings of leisure are also the meanings of work. People in talking about their work say that they get all the satisfactions from work that they might get from leisure except that of a change from work. In comparing these meanings Havighurst states a general principle of the *equivalence of work and play*: to a considerable extent people can get the same satisfactions from leisure as from work. There are, of course, limitations to this principle. For instance, a person who has found friends at work and who values sociability with these friends may have very little further need for sociability during his leisure time. But when he retires he may find sociability in a non-work setting and thus substitute leisure for work satisfactorily, provided the other positive meanings that work had for him can also be continued by substitute activities. Happy retirement depends on the previous life a person has led, as well as on the physical and social conditions in which he finds himself at this point in his life.

In a further report Havighurst and Feigenbaum related leisure activity to social role performance.[24] They distinguished two general patterns of life-style and leisure; community-centred and home-centred. They noted that these two patterns appeared to be equally accessible to middle-class people but that working-class people were rarely community-centred. In about five per cent of cases life-style and leisure style were not in close relation: these were people who invested most of their energy in work or in home and children, with little time and inclination for leisure. Another six per cent had a high level of leisure activity, but were dissatisfied or inadequate workers, parents or spouses who attempted to compensate with a high leisure performance.

In this chapter we have considered the functions, activities and meanings involved in leisure. Three general conclusions emerge. First, the functions which leisure has for the structure and pattern of society are related to those apparent in the lives of its individual members. Secondly, ways of spending leisure time tend to vary with the demands and satisfactions of the occupation. And thirdly, the meanings found in leisure and the attachment to home or community appear to be different for sex and social class groups. In the next chapter we shall consider in greater detail the mutual influence of work and leisure.

6 Work and Leisure Today

Having reviewed research findings and observations relevant to the separate spheres of work and leisure, we may now turn to the ways in which each affects the other. There is no strict dividing line between the separate studies of work and leisure and of the work–leisure relationship, but just as the previous two chapters concentrated on the former, this chapter will concentrate on the latter. The work and leisure patterns characteristic of certain occupational groups are first considered, followed by a brief survey of the industrial recreation movement. Work and leisure as alternative sources of central life interest are then discussed, and the chapter concludes with an assessment of the pros and cons in the 'fusion-versus-polarity' debate.

Group Patterns

The studies quoted in the previous chapter were fairly straightforward accounts of the ways in which people in certain occupations or class groups typically spend their leisure time. A functional relationship may be inferred from some of the patterns of leisure – for example, the greater need for non-work exercise by white-collar workers – but we may turn to a further group of studies for a more explicit treatment of the work-leisure relationship.

Data are available on the relation between work and leisure characteristic of a wide variety of occupational groups. To consider first the manual group; the decreased physical strain of work has brought about a change in the function of leisure for some manual workers. Thus it has been observed that the jobs of steel-workers have now become so relatively lacking in strain that the worker leaves the plant with a good deal of energy left which carries him readily through his leisure hours. However, in occupations like mining and fishing leisure tends to have a more traditional role. Jeremy Tunstall's study of distant-water fishermen showed that leisure during the three months in the year they are ashore fulfils the functions of status seeking and of explosive compensation for physically damaging work.[1]

Something of this violent reaction to work can be seen in the leisure activities of some non-manual workers. Friedmann quotes a study of the leisure habits of employees at the Postal Cheque Centre in Paris, whose jobs are completely routine: on leaving the office, these clerks are either much more active or, in contrast, withdraw into themselves, in a sort of apathy.[2] But a different pattern of work and leisure is shown by those non-manual employees whose work demands more involvement and responsibility. Among professional engineers studied by Gerstl and Hutton, twenty-three per cent said they had hobbies connected with the field of engineering, and as many as seventy-three per cent claimed work-connected reading as one of their hobby interests.[3]

Heckscher and DeGrazia concluded from their survey that the way of life of American business executives permits no clear-cut distinction between work and leisure.[4] To counteract the encroachment of work on leisure time, the executive's work is penetrated by qualities which we would ordinarily associate with leisure. On the other hand, David Riesman remarks that the professional or business person is apt to leave his work with a good many tensions created by his reactions to interpersonal situations, and so he may have to satisfy his leisure 'needs' before he can rise from the level of re-creation to the level of creation.[5] He may move from a job where he is constantly faced with others and their expectations to leisure pursuits, again in the company of others, where workmanlike performance is also expected of him.

The penetration of the businessman's work into the rest of his life is a function of the demands of the work itself rather than of the culture. This is illustrated by the close similarity of the Japanese businessman's life to that of the American's. Ezra Vogel reports that in Japan business is combined with community activities, recreation and personal activities.[6] It is difficult to distinguish working time from leisure time, and the businessman often entertains his clients with a trip to the golf course or a party with entertainment by geisha girls. Vogel also notes that, like successful businessmen, doctors rarely make a sharp separation between work and leisure, partly because to some extent working hours are determined by the arrival of patients. It is the salaried man who makes the sharpest distinction between working time and free time. In contrast to the businessman who mixes business and leisure, and to the doctor whose leisure is determined by the absence of patients, the salaried man generally has set hours so that he can plan certain hours of the day and certain days of the week for himself and his family.

The type of leisure activity chosen may reflect the type of work and work situation. Even differences in *style* of a given type of leisure activity may be related to work experience. Thus K. P. Etzkorn notes that 'public campground' camping, which is routinized, is practised more by individuals with routinized jobs, while 'wilderness' camping is preferred by individuals in more creative occupations.[7] Fred Blum goes more deeply into the relation between work and leisure experienced by the typical packing-house worker.[8] This type of worker has a tendency to carry work attitudes on into the week-end in spite of a strong psychological fatigue and desire to get away from work and everything it stands for. Since it is almost impossible to work eight hours intensively and switch over suddenly to a new, creative way of life, workers are pushed into some kind of activity which keeps them occupied without reminding them of their work. Fishing is one of the favourite pastimes of these workers. It has elements which are just the opposite of the work process – relaxing, being outdoors, getting 'away from it all'.

And yet it has elements akin to the work process: It does not require any initiative or attention and, most of all, it allows the psychological mechanisms of busy-ness to go on. It makes it possible to carry an essential attitude growing out of the work process into the leisure time without making its experience in any way similar to the experience of work . . . it eliminates the necessity of a basic change in attitude, of effort and attention.

Industrial Recreation

Industrial recreation is a term used to describe those recreational activities which are provided to satisfy the particular needs and tastes of employees of business and industrial firms. Industrial sports clubs (or sports and social clubs) have grown up largely during the last sixty years, and it is estimated that there are now around 1,300 industrial clubs in the United Kingdom. All types of employees are members of these clubs but, according to one survey,[9] of all sports club members (private and works), higher proportions of manual workers belong only to works clubs than do professional and other non-manual workers. Other surveys show that working-class people are less often members of voluntary associations than are middle-class people, and the 'middle-class' nature of the private clubs probably accounts for the higher proportion of manual workers in works clubs only.

An association has been shown between being an efficient worker and participating more than the average in recreational activities, although it is difficult to say which is cause and which is effect. In many companies recreation has become a most effective tool in developing better communication between labour and management. It is claimed that both management and labour recognize the place of recreation in the industrial pattern through the provision for and by the workers of 'wholesome' leisure interests. Such provision is said to benefit the industrial world because it breaks down barriers, relieves job monotony, builds friendships, helps to cut absenteeism, improves the general morale, strengthens public relations and improves community relations.

The advantages accruing to the employer from a programme of industrial recreation have been candidly set out by T. Yukawa:

... off-hour habits and behaviour have an important bearing on job performance ... Recreation combats job monotony by providing mental and physical relaxation, toning up the employee, before and after work and during lunch periods. .... A recreation program is especially valuable in helping new employees become adjusted to their jobs. They swing more easily and willingly into the rhythm of their work when they discover the friendly atmosphere surrounding it. .... Recreation often exposes leadership qualifications which an employee has no chance to demonstrate on the job. .... Thus recreation may be used as an evaluation tool to screen employees qualified for promotion. Best of all, this screening is done at times when the employee is least aware he is being observed. ... When a company becomes known as a 'good place to work' it has no difficulty attracting employees or holding them. An organized recreation program builds stronger employee loyalty . . .[10]

The campaign for industrial recreation seems to be concerned with the worker from two aspects – his moral welfare and his physical condition. On the one hand, J. M. Anderson claims that 'in many areas where organized recreation programmes have not been made available to employees, the workers are engaging in widespread dissipation.'[11] On the other hand, T. Woody remarks that industrialized societies are giving increased scientific study to leisure recreations to alleviate the stress and strain of particular occupations.[12] The interest is not just in leisure time away from the work situation but also during breaks at work. Peter Cullen reports that in many European countries management has introduced 'break' gymnastics or work-bench callisthenics, and this kind of tension-releasing activity has apparently been well received by employees.[13] Although such activity may have a leisure-like quality, its function in the industrial process and the fact that it can scarcely be said to be freely chosen put it in the category of work obligations rather than of leisure.

There is some evidence of a diminishing interest in industrial recreation on the part of both management and workers. Management is not quite so sure as it was about the place of sport and welfare in industry today, while in the clubs apathy seems to predominate among the membership. There has been a considerable growth in opportunities for recreation generally, and the motor car and television have altered leisure habits. Also, management is becoming increasingly convinced that the structural determinants of behaviour at work – organizational structure, control systems, pay methods, and the like – are more important than personal relationships and welfare. Most workers today like to seek their recreation and self-realization outside the work milieu. Despite the fact that large organizations, which are in a better position than smaller ones to provide recreation facilities, are employing proportionately greater numbers of people, it may well be that the whole industrial recreation movement has passed its peak.

Central Life Interest

We can learn much about the nature of the relationship between work and leisure from the relative values which people place on these two spheres of life. Robert Dubin has coined the term 'central life interest' to refer to a significant area of social experience.[14] Assuming that social participation in a sphere may be necessary but not important to an individual, he classified replies by industrial workers to a series of three-choice questions as job-oriented, non-job-oriented, or indifferent. The results showed that by a margin of three to one work was not in general a central life interest for the industrial workers sampled. This was most strongly the case with informal relations and personal satisfactions, though work was the majority choice for organizational and technological relations. Louis Orzack gave an amended version of Dubin's schedule to a sample of professional nurses, and his results confirmed the prediction that professionals would be much more oriented to work as a central life interest than would industrial workers.[15] By nearly four to one the nurses gave overall 'work' replies, and only in the case of informal relations was the non-work sphere slightly preferred.

Subsequent research on the subject of central life interest has focused mainly on manual workers. Arthur Kornhauser reported that the job was chosen as the most satisfying part of life by only two per cent of routine production workers compared with nine per cent of other factory men.[16] Lafitte found that the engagements into which Australian factory workers put their major efforts varied considerably, but were chiefly outside work.[17] The worker, he concluded, may be family-centred or self-centred, but he is never work-centred. Dumazedier asked a sample of workers in the French town of Annecy which activities gave them most satisfaction.[18] Of unskilled workers twenty-five per cent replied 'leisure', forty-seven per cent 'family' and twenty-four per cent 'work'. Of skilled workers twenty-five per cent replied 'leisure', fifty-three per cent 'family', and only fifteen per cent 'work'.

A study going more deeply into the central life interest of various types of industrial worker is reported by Kunio Odaka.[19] Five Japanese companies were included in the survey, which involved several thousand employees. Respondents were asked to choose from a list of items the one which they felt contributed most to making their life worth living. The most popular answer was 'making a happy home' (36–56%), followed by 'leisure' (25–47%), with 'work at the company' a poor third (6–14%). Another question sought to classify workers' preferences among 'five types of living related to work and leisure'. These were defined as:

(a) *work-oriented-unilateral* ('Work is man's duty. I wish to devote myself wholly to my work without any thought of leisure.')
(b) *leisure-oriented-unilateral* ('Work is no more than a means for living. The enjoyment of leisure is what makes human life worth living.')
(c) *identity* ('There is no distinction between work and leisure. I therefore have no need of being liberated from work in order that I may enjoy leisure.')
(d) *split* ('Work is work and leisure is leisure. Modern man gets his work done smartly, and enjoys his leisure moderately.')
(e) *integrated* ('Work makes leisure pleasurable, and leisure gives new energy to work. I wish to work with all my might, and to enjoy leisure.')

The replies of more than 600 employees in one manufacturing company were analysed according to their type of work in the company:

	(a) Work-oriented-unilateral	(b) Leisure-oriented-unilateral	(c) Identity	(d) Split	(e) Integrated	Others and Unknown	Total
	%	%	%	%	%	%	%
Temporary Operative	15	12	15	18	38	3	101
Regular Operative	8	5	8	25	53	1	100
Supervisory	18	3	5	24	49	2	101
Administrative	22	4	4	22	48	–	100
Technical	23	7	7	7	55	2	101
Whole Company	12	5	7	23	51	2	100

With one or two exceptions, the distribution of replies according to type of work was fairly similar. It must be borne in mind, however, that all the respondents were in one company and this may have had the effect of narrowing differences which a survey including a wider range of occupations might have revealed. One problem of interpreting data of this kind is that one does not know the extent to which the 'right' as opposed to the true answers were given by respondents. Certainly the majority verdict in favour of the 'integrated' pattern, in which the work ingredient is presumably as highly valued as the leisure, seems to conflict with the much more popular choice of non-work than of work as what makes life worth living.

Fusion Versus Polarity

The type of relationship existing between work and leisure spheres is to be seen at both the societal and individual levels. We may first consider the arguments for and against the proposition that work and leisure are becoming similar to each other. At the societal level the evidence for both 'fusion' and 'polarity' consists of changes that have allegedly taken place in the content of work, the way it is organized and the setting in which it is done. At the individual level fusion would be experienced as spillover of work and leisure spheres and polarity as opposition, or at least differentiation, of these spheres.

Wilensky cites as evidence of work–leisure fusion the long coffee break among white-collar girls, the lunch 'hour' among top business and professional people, card games among night shift employees; and off work, the do-it-yourself movement, spare-time jobs, 'customers' golf' for sales executives, and commuter-train conferences for account executives.[20] Also, many devices are being invented for creating spaces of free time within the working day and at intervals throughout the career. In America the sabbatical year is no longer exclusive to academic employees. One firm has for some time been granting twelve months' paid holiday after ten years of service and steelworkers have the chance of a quarter-sabbatical – three months off after five years' service. Another type of work–leisure fusion, the integration of sex into work, is noted by Herbert Marcuse: 'Without ceasing to be an instrument of labor, the body is allowed to exhibit its sexual features in the everyday work world and in work relations.'[21]

No doubt with such evidence as this in mind, Gregory Stone has asserted that 'more and more we work at our play and play at our work ... our play is disguised by work and vice versa. Consequently, we begin to evaluate our leisure time in terms of the potential it has for work – for us to "do it ourselves", and we evaluate our work in terms of the potential it has for play.'[22] Riesman and Blomberg extend this point by maintaining that leisure now gives status to work rather than the other way round.[23] Young workers look to non-work activities for a more personal as well as more portable kind of status. They are judged, as it were, 'horizontally' by their style of life rather than vertically by their occupation.

Riesman attempts to explain this work–leisure fusion in terms of the 'changing American character' from inner-directedness to other-directedness: 'The other-directed person has no clear core of self to escape from; no clear line between production and consumption; between adjusting to the group and serving private interests; between work and play.'[24] Yet other-directedness is not so much a type of character as a mode of adjustment to technological civilization. The aspect of leisure that is most amenable to fusion with work is mass culture, because it is most subject to social control and therefore can be made most 'functional' to the industrial system as a whole. Irving Howe sees this process of manipulation clearly:

... except during brief revolutionary intervals, the quality of leisure time activity cannot vary too sharply from that of the work day. If it did the office or factory worker would be exposed to those terrible dualities that make it so difficult for the intellectual to adjust his job to himself. But the worker wants no part of such difficulties, he has enough already. Following the dictum of industrial society that anonymity is a key to safety, he seeks the least troublesome solution: mass culture. Whatever its manifest content, mass culture must therefore not subvert the basic patterns of industrial life. Leisure time must be so organized as to bear a factitious relationship to working time: apparently different, actually the same. It must provide relief from work monotony without making the return to work too unbearable ...[25]

The popular game of bingo is a good example. Bingo has several features which are similar to the work experience of many of those who take part in it: it involves concentration, regulated patterns of physical movement, is supervised by someone else, and allows breaks for refreshments.

There are other observers, however, who take a different view about what has been happening to work and leisure. Dismissing evidence of fusion such as that cited above as marginal to the main structure of modern industry, they seek to show that work has become more concentratedly and actively work. It may be less arduous physically than it used to be, but its present standards of efficiency are said to require one to key oneself to a higher pitch of nervous and mental effort. The theme of alienation from work is relevant here, since it implies that work as a sphere of human experience is estranged from other spheres such as that of leisure. Under conditions of present society, it is said, the 'break in consciousness' between work and socialized play, begun during the industrial revolution, has been completed. Certainly it is arguable that the institution of employment has brought about a fairly sharp distinction between working life and private life, between sold time and unsold time. The 'evasion of work', according to Daniel Bell, is the characteristic fact about work in the life of a contemporary American:

Work is irksome, and if it cannot be evaded it can be reduced. In the old days the shadings between work and leisure were hard to distinguish. In modern life the ideal is to minimize the unpleasant aspects of work as much as possible by pleasant distractions (wall colors, music, rest periods) and to hasten away as quickly as possible, uncontaminated by work and unimpaired by its arduousness ... [26]

The ideal may be to split the unsatisfying life of work from the more rewarding life of non-work, but we must reserve judgment on the extent to which this ideal is actually being achieved.

The evidence for fusion or polarity of work and leisure at the societal level is conflicting, and the theories built on selections of it are not easily reconcilable. Perhaps the whole argument has been confused by referring to different levels – that of society in general and that of occupations and work milieux in particular – each of which requires its own methods of analysis and conclusions. There is the further point that fusion and polarity may not exhaust all the possibilities of relationship between work and leisure. The concepts of fusion and polarity are essentially *dynamic* ones referring to a process of change in a relationship. They also denote *symbiotic* relationships, in the sense that each side of the relationship is dependent for its form on the form of the other – by a process, as it were, of positive attraction or negative repulsion. This leaves a third possibility: that the nature of the 'relationship' between work and leisure may be non-symbiotic, i.e. that work and leisure may each have 'lives of their own' and be *relatively* unaffected by each other.

In the final three chapters we shall examine further the theoretical and practical implications of these three types of work–leisure relationship. But before that the next chapter will describe the results of my research findings which bear on this issue.

7 Some Studies of Particular Groups

This chapter brings together the findings relevant to work and leisure of a series of surveys undertaken or participated in by the writer. These surveys covered other topics besides work and leisure, the findings of which are not dealt with here. Technical details about the samples, methods used to carry out the surveys, tests of statistical significance, and so on, are given elsewhere.[1]

(a) Business and Service Workers

My first fieldwork designed to include the study of work and leisure consisted of 200 pilot interviews with people employed in 'business' and 'service' occupations. I wanted to start with occupations that were likely to have markedly different influences on the people working in them. My two groups were adapted from Blau and Scott's categories of business and service *organizations*, representing respectively organizations where the owners are the prime beneficiaries and those where the client group is the prime beneficiary.[2] The two groups of occupations were known to differ in the content of the work and the way it was organized, and at this stage these were the main variables to be related to people's feelings about their jobs.

Psychologists maintain that people of certain personality types and with certain attitudes tend to seek out occupations that suit their personalities and attitudes. Research on the interests of people entering certain occupations or training courses confirms that this is generally the case. Thus prospective businessmen tend to be interested in money and leisure, prospective social workers in the welfare of others, and so on.[3] Without denying the importance of personality factors in the initial *choice* of an occupation, I wanted to concentrate on a rather different question: to what extent does the experience and meaning of work, and the work-leisure relationship vary for people in different kinds of occupation? I also had in mind the possibility that occupations might shape the personalities and attitudes of those who stay in them for any length of time.

Asked what was the thing about their work that gave them most *satisfaction*, sixty-nine per cent of the service workers mentioned something to do with their clients, compared with twenty-four per cent of business workers who mentioned something to do with their customers. Part of this difference was accounted for by the service people more often having client contact as a major part of their work than the business people had customer contact. But even when the 'non-contact' group was removed from the analysis, an occupational difference still remained. This indicates that while personal contact with those other than colleagues is a major source of satisfaction to people whose jobs entail this contact, more satisfaction is found in the client relationship than in the customer relationship.

Autonomy in the work situation was measured by the extent to which informants felt that they could determine or help to determine the decisions or details connected with their jobs. The service people (76%) much more often reported having autonomy than did the business people (44%). Much of the difference in autonomy between the occupational groups is explained by the different systems of management in the typical business concern and in the typical service organization. A business organization is more likely to be what Burns and Stalker call 'mechanistic', features of it including specialization of tasks, hierarchical control, and frequent interaction between superior and subordinate.[4] On the other hand, a service organization is more likely to be 'organic' – all its members doing the same sort of work, and featuring control by small groups, and frequent interaction between colleagues. The typical service job which consists of interviewing clients and helping to solve their personal problems can best be done with a maximum of individual discretion and a minimum of subjection to personal authority. But business efficiency is aided, at least up to a point, by bureaucracy and formal organization, and a consequent reduction of the area of individual discretion. Much of the autonomy found on the business side occurs where the work consists of dealing with people, and much of the feeling of lack of autonomy on the service side arises from administrative demands. The latter situation is well illustrated by a young woman youth employment officer's remark: 'I have settled down to do things the way I want within the red tape.'

On the assumption that the degree to which a person feels 'used' or *extended* in his job is related to his other work experiences and attitudes, the question was asked, 'How much of your abilities and potentialities do you use in your work?' The business people more often said they were limited by lack of scope than did the service people, but the difference was barely significant. There was a clearer trend to being limited by work pressures on the service side: ten out of the twelve people who reported this kind of limitation were in service occupations. This figure does not represent all those experiencing work pressures, but only those who found that these pressures affected the quality of the work they were able to do, and hence their potential used. This often happened where case-loads were too heavy to allow much intensive case-work with individuals. As one young almoner put it, 'It's the days with perhaps four patients that bring out the most in you. With a quantity of patients you are worn out, but in a different way.'

A question on type of *involvement* in work allowed informants to choose 'self-expression', 'a way to earn', or 'both' as describing their own involvement. Among service informants sixty-seven per cent chose self-expression, compared with only thirty-six per cent among business informants. This difference is largely attributable to what is often called a vocational attitude to jobs in the service category. Although both types of occupation include those which provide services, the main object of the business concern is to make money, while the main object of the service organization is to provide the service. It is not surprising, therefore, that employees in each type of occupation should reflect in their type of work involvement the main object of their employing body. A mosaic of the typical 'service' point of view shows how deep involvement can go:

This job is a means of contributing socially; it consolidates my life and is part of settling down. ... In this type of work we are doing things on a broad scale – one feels it is a bit of social history in the making ... I once got out of social work and missed it terribly. I felt guilty about having an easier job ... This occupation is not just a means of earning or passing the time. It is difficult to visualize life without it . . . Work is now organizing my life instead of I organizing the work.'

On the other hand, the 'business' mosaic is less inner-directed and contains quite a strong feeling of being carried along with the majority:

It's mainly a way of earning a living. Few people can see it otherwise . . . Most people, if they were honest, would say they work for money. . . . As you get older with more family responsibilities it becomes more like earning a living. . . . It's certainly not expressing yourself, writing little figures in books. . . . You are caught and put in the cage so early you can't do much about it.'

A further measure of occupational involvement is whether a person's present job is the one he would *choose* under other conditions. The question was put: 'If you could choose any occupation regardless of money which one would you choose?' Nearly three-quarters of the service people would still prefer their present occupation or something allied to it, compared with only thirty per cent of the business people. There was considerably more reluctance on the service side to consider changing jobs, or even to admit the existence of choice. 'I see life as living, as involvement rather than choosing this or that,' as one young male youth employment officer put it. Sometimes the reason given for not desiring change was a practical one – 'this is the field in which I have most experience' – and sometimes a value judgment was made of the work itself. The remark of a female mental welfare officer, 'I couldn't do anything else – I wouldn't feel it was real work', seems to be a view held by many whose work has a clear social purpose.

Several questions were put on aspects of the work–leisure relationship. With Dubin's concept of *central life interest* in mind,[5] informants were asked 'What is your main interest in life?' and their answers were coded into broad categories. Among the business people only eleven per cent gave 'work' answers, compared with twenty-nine per cent of service people; seventy-eight per cent of business and thirty-nine per cent of service people gave 'non-work' answers, and eleven per cent of business and thirty-two per cent of service people said they had no main interest. The interviews produced evidence that at least some of the business occupations, especially banking and insurance, are not regarded as socially useful by many of the people who work in them. Service occupations, however, are usually regarded as socially important by their employees. This, plus the difference in type of involvement in work, could account for most of the business-service differences found in work as a central life interest.

Informants were asked whether they had as *close friends* any of the people they worked with. Of those in business occupations fifty-seven per cent said 'none', compared with only twenty-two per cent of those in service occupations. The explanation of this probably lies in the differences in objective work situations and in values attached to work. In many service occupations having friends in other jobs is in effect, if not in intention, discouraged. As one child care officer put it, 'This job makes outside contacts difficult to keep up because you can't rely on being able to keep evening appointments.'

Answers to the question 'Do you find that your work *encroaches* on your free time?' were classified as 'a lot', 'a little' or 'never'. Among the business informants, sixty-eight per cent said 'never', compared with only thirty-six per cent among service informants. It was made clear to informants that the question was not concerned with irregular hours of work or overtime, but with voluntary activities connected with work, such as meetings and work-connected reading. The nature of the work seems to be an important factor in the extent of its spillover into free time. It is possible to let almost any job encroach on free time, but some types of work lend themselves to spillover and some do not. Thus a technical college lecturer said 'I am always having to consider the next day's work or the next term's work, thinking about and preparing for classes.' But an insurance man, even with working hours often outside nine-to-five, was able to say 'When I'm at home the iron curtain is dropped so far as work is concerned.'

Another phase of the analysis was to find out how far certain answers were correlated. It emerged that a cluster of variables was associated with the service occupations: having autonomy in the work situation, being fully extended in the job, having a self-expressive involvement in work, having central life interest in work, having work colleagues as close friends, and letting work encroach on leisure. The business occupations were associated with the negative of these variables – not having autonomy in the work situation, and so on.

An index of 'work involvement' composed of these items was applied to each of the ten occupational samples. Results suggested that of the occupations studied, child care, mental welfare, teaching and almoning produce the greatest degree of work involvement as measured by the index, and banking, insurance, advertising and retail selling the least involvement. The occupations associated with high work involvement are all service occupations concerned with the problems and development of people; the occupations associated with low work involvement are business ones concerned with impersonal things or with personal relations on a business basis. The intermediate position of accountancy and youth employment is of special interest. Some of the accountants in the sample were working on their own account and retained some of the classic professional-client relationship, while the youth employment officers tended to feel themselves partly in the business world and partly in the social work world. Features of these two occupations draw attention to other occupations which are marginal between business and service: performing characteristically business work for a service organization, and vice versa. A few supplementary interviews with people in such jobs – including an accountant working for a government body, and an interviewer in an employment agency – indicated that they had a 'split' attitude to their jobs, separating the service from the business element.

The results of these pilot interviews confirmed the initial hypothesis that people working in the business and service occupations differed markedly in their degree of work involvement. The results were also used to select three of the ten specific occupations for more intensive study and to provide a test of some of the questions to be used in that study.

(b) Banking, Youth Employment, Child Care and Manual Workers

From the pilot interviews, child care officers were found to be one of the most work-involved groups and bank employees one of the least work-involved. Larger samples of these two groups, together with youth employment officers, who had an intermediate position on the scale, were sent questionnaires by post. A shorter version of the questionnaire was also sent to a mixed sample of manual workers, but for various reasons this must be regarded as a preliminary enquiry.[6] Altogether, 425 people cooperated by returning usable forms.

The scope of the inquiry was the same as that of the pilot interviews, plus some questions on the amount and use of leisure time. The results of questions which were the same as, or similar to, those put in the pilot interviews generally confirmed that child care officers are typical of 'service' workers and bank employees of 'business' workers. The youth employment people gave answers generally more like those of child care officers than those of bank employees, thus confirming their kinship with the former as 'service' workers. The distribution of answers to other questions was as follows.

Information on *use of abilities* was gained from two questions, one on the number of abilities and the other on the extent to which they were used. Three in five of the youth employment and child care respondents, two in five of the manual workers, but only one in five of the bank employees, felt that they used most of their abilities in their job. Very small proportions of youth employment and child care people felt that they used only a few of their abilities, but twenty-eight per cent of bank employees and twenty-five per cent of manual workers felt this. Nearly three-quarters of bank respondents felt that they used their abilities in only a superficial or general way, compared with nearly half the youth employment sample and less than a third of the child care sample. Manual workers were not asked this question.

A different measure of job *autonomy* was used compared with that in the pilot interviews. Respondents were asked to say which of three methods of decision applied when changes had to be made or difficult problems solved in their jobs. In all three occupations the method most frequently reported was 'superior would decide after consultation with staff'. The second most frequent method given by youth employment and child care respondents was the more autonomous 'decision taken at a meeting of all involved'. On the other hand, the less autonomous method, 'superior would decide without consultation with staff', was given by a third of the bank people but by very few of the others. A few respondents in all occupations said that the decision was 'their own'.

Several questions were asked about the use of leisure. Concerning membership of non-work *organizations*, two-thirds of the youth employment and child care samples were active (holding office or being regular attenders) in at least one such organization, compared with half the bank employees and a third of the manual workers. A breakdown of type of organization membership showed that people in the three non-manual occupations were equally active in recreational organizations (about four in ten had at least one active membership) but among manual workers this proportion fell to one in ten. There was also a large occupational difference in membership of non-recreational organizations. This indicates that non-work obligations are more onerous for youth employment and child care employees than for those in banking and manual work.

Respondents were asked how many *hours of leisure* they normally had per week. It was clear that definitions of what constitutes leisure vary considerably. A few respondents who reported having 100–130 hours of leisure each week had obviously deducted working and work-related time from the total week of 168 hours. At the other end of the scale, six respondents said they had six or few hours of leisure each week. However, two-thirds of all respondents stated their weekly hours of leisure at a figure between 25 and 50. The average weekly hours of leisure reported by youth employment and child care employees were 33–34 and by bank and manual workers 42–43. There were very small differences in the leisure time of men and women and of the married and the single in the sample.

Something about *leisure preferences* was discovered by asking 'If you had an extra two hours each day, how would you prefer to spend them?' Some interesting occupational differences emerged. The bank people much less often preferred reading, and more often chose out-of-doors and sporting activities or to relax or sleep. The manual workers had the most 'home-centred' choices, partly because they had the highest proportion of married informants. The differences in the choice of work or study were small, but from comments made by youth employment and child care people about the type of reading which would be chosen it appears that this is often background reading to the job.

Respondents were asked about their *reasons for enjoying leisure*. They were given the alternatives: 'Because it satisfies the interests that you *would like* to satisfy in your work, because it is satisfying in a *different way* from your work, or because it is *completely different* from your work?' Most respondents chose the second or third alternatives, possibly because the idea behind the first is not clear. The bank people most often said 'because it is completely different from work' and the youth employment and child care people 'because it is satisfying in a different way from work'. The typical banking answer indicates a greater polarization of leisure and work as satisfying and un-satisfying, while the other answer indicates that both leisure and work are found satisfying in their different ways.

Information on *how different from work* respondents felt their leisure to be was obtained from the choice among: completely different, a lot of free time taken up by things connected with work, or a little free time taken up by things connected with work. About three-quarters of the bank and manual workers said that their leisure was completely different from their work, as against a quarter of the youth employment people, and a third of the child care people. Nearly a third of the youth employment and child care workers claimed that matters con-nected with work took up a lot of their free time, but only very small proportions of the bank and manual workers said this.

The groups using most of many of their abilities in their jobs were compared on two non-work questions with those using only a few of their abilities. The former were more likely to be active in, or members of, at least one non-work organization (78%) than were those who used only a few of their abilities (57%). A higher proportion (25%) of those using most or many of their abilities would prefer to spend extra free time reading or studying than would those using only a few abilities (9%). These last two findings have special implications for the claim that those who fail to find self-expression and a sense of achievement in their work may turn to non-work life to find it. The present evidence is that those who find work more demanding of their abilities are more likely to be socially or intellectually active in their leisure than are those who find work less demanding. Non-involvement in work seems more likely to discourage than to facilitate involvement in leisure.

A question put only to manual workers concerned the *meaning of leisure*. Pilot inquiries showed that most people agreed with one of three types of definition, and these were put on the schedule. By arrangement, Dr Swift also included this question in his interviews with paid social workers.[7] The manual workers in the sample differed very little from the social workers in their answers: seventy-three per cent of manual workers (77% of social workers) thought leisure meant 'only the time you feel free to do whatever you like; sixteen per cent (14%) thought it meant 'all the time you are not actually at work', and eleven per cent (5%) 'all the time except when working or doing essential things like eating and sleeping'. This suggests that most people tend to define leisure in a positive rather than a residual way and it confirms the dimensions ('time' and 'feeling free') which our earlier definition embraced.

There was a tendency among manual workers for those who thought their work was skilled and who used most of their abilities in their job to define leisure more often as freedom than did those who thought their work was less skilled and used fewer of their abilities. One possible explanation of this difference is that the residual definitions indicate a polarity of work and leisure. They are, therefore, more likely to be chosen by those who have a negative or neutral attitude to work. It may, however, be argued that the 'positive' response implies that freedom is obtainable only in leisure, and therefore that those who experience some degree of freedom in their work should be inclined to reject this definition. Perhaps those who are in skilled jobs using most of their abilities *do* feel less free, in the sense of being more committed to their work. More definite conclusions on these points must await further research.

To sum up, there seem to be two broad patterns of work and leisure experiences and attitudes among the groups sampled. On the one hand, people in banking and the less skilled kinds of manual jobs are comparatively uninvolved in their work, 'privatised' in their leisure, and polar in their conceptions of work and leisure. On the other hand, the youth employment, child care, and to some extent the skilled manual workers are involved in their work, more socially and intellectually active in their leisure, and have a more integrated conception of work and leisure. These are tentative and very broad conclusions and (especially in the case of manual workers) based on research that needs to be repeated and expanded. But they point to the pervasive influences of work on non-work experiences and cast doubt on the theory that people can make up in leisure for what they lack in work.

(c) Residential Social Workers

Almost by definition, social workers are more dedicated to their work than are people in most other occupations. But the small group of social workers who both live and work on the same premises are even more removed from the ordinary conditions of nine-to-five jobs than are non-residential social workers. For the former, work and leisure do not have the same meaning or the same separateness that they have for most other people. In an attempt to find out more about the way residential social workers pattern their lives, six case studies were carried out with various types of informant.

(1)

Mr A., a middle-aged bachelor, is the director of a trust, the main function of which is to run a community for the homeless and destitute, a large proportion of whom are meths drinkers. In order to establish and maintain a proper human relationship with every person who comes for assistance, Mr A. and his associates identify themselves to a large extent with those they are trying to help. They think of themselves, equally, as 'misfits' and refer to the 'square world' of the outside: Mr A. is completely dedicated to his very demanding work. His activities are of two main kinds: dealing with the men, including organizing the community and sending out teams to bring into the community those in need of help; and the public relations effort of getting support for the work, including maintaining active contact with other social services to their mutual benefit.

Leisure in the accepted sense is non-existent in Mr A.'s life. His only diversion is a weekly visit to his ageing mother in the country. He has no urge to use part of his time away from his work situation to escape its demands or its stresses. Relaxation is necessary to him, but this does not imply withdrawal. 'I am relaxing now – I relax when I am with the men in the evening. ...'

(2)

Mr B. is a Church social worker. Those who have personal problems may receive advice from him in the form of counselling or befriending. The unit is manned by a small non-residential staff and Mr B. is the only member who has living quarters on the premises, to which access is had only through the office. Each evening at eleven the phone is switched through to his apartment and he alone deals with night calls.

Mr B. is unmarried and his friends are mostly social workers or men of the Church. He rarely goes to parties or places of entertainment except when accompanying a friend or client, but he feels that he leads quite a full social life through his work. His occasional day off is not the conventional day away from the work situation. It simply consists in announcing to the office staff that he is having a day off, so that if he happens not to be available they can tell callers this. Otherwise it appears that his days off are very much the same as other days.

He can give no estimate of how much leisure he normally has, nor even of what to count as leisure. 'I am in my room of an evening and the vicar comes to call. We chat about various matters. He represents my employer but he is also my friend. I don't know whether to call this work or leisure.' He identifies 'free time' with time during which he is not committed to see anyone. Asked about his hobbies, he will give a characteristic answer: 'My hobbies are psychopaths and alcoholics. ...'

(3)

Father C. is an elderly Catholic priest. In addition to the usual duties of a priest, he has assumed many other civic duties. He lives in the presbytery attached to the church and is assisted by another priest.

Father C. believes in being 'approachable and available' to those who need him. 'For my leisure I work, for my play I work, my hobby is work. The one thing that keeps me from cracking up is variety – different people, each with their different problems. . . .' He is entitled to a regular day off each week but does not take this. If he has to visit a country or seaside town for a conference or meeting he will take a few hours off to relax while there. But he never takes such a trip for the purpose of leisure alone.

Does he have any free time? 'Yes – between appointments.' But the working day is so full that there is usually very little such free time. He has many close friends in all walks of life. He agrees that he has a good social life, but says this is mainly in the course of his work. He regards making speeches, which he is often called upon to do, not as a chore but as a convivial activity. It is probably this unserious attitude to many of his duties that enables him to live almost entirely within the realm of work.

(4)

Mr D. is the administrator-cum-warden of a residential hostel housing forty or so men, who come from various sources including prisons and mental hospitals. He has two assistants, plus four on the domestic staff. He has a wife and three small children and they live in a flat upstairs.

Mr D. leads a remarkably busy life. There were periods in the past when he was without assistants, and as his two present ones are young and fairly inexperienced, the men prefer to come to him with their problems. So the time that he is 'free' in a realistic sense is rare. The residents are fairly understanding, but there is nearly always someone who needs attention. Whether or not he is 'off duty', he will make time to attend to these people, and it is not uncommon for him and his wife to be called upon when in their own quarters.

'I am not really an organized man,' says Mr D., though not as a point of pride. The house is like a large family home where people address each other by their christian names. There is a remarkably relaxed atmosphere around Mr D., which belies the heavy burdens of his work. 'By nature I am a man of leisure,' he says, 'and leisure is very important to me.'

(5)

Miss E. is matron of a small mother and baby home. She has an assistant and a small part-time staff. Her work is varied and includes keeping records as well as looking after the twenty or so mothers and their children. Officially she has one full and two half days off a week, but since the home is understaffed she often uses the half days to catch up on necessary paper work. She admits that she spends a lot of time talking with her friends about her work, but one or two of them are not at all interested in it and she thinks this is a good thing, as it gives her a wider horizon.

'You have to give your whole life to this sort of work,' she says, with a touch of regret. When she was assistant matron she used to attend evening classes, but with increased responsibilities she had to give those up. Today she has nothing she would call hobbies or spare-time interests. In addition to her own room upstairs she has a sitting-room which she shares with her assistant and next to this a small office. She can relax in the sitting-room, but is quite often disturbed by the phone or by someone wanting to see her. Since her working day often consists of fourteen hours on duty, she takes whatever breaks she can between doing things and seeing people.

(6)

Mr F. is a young man who used to be in the business world and has only recently begun in the field of social work. He is employed in a rehabilitation centre with over thirty residents. He is reluctant to use the word 'vocational' about his work. He seems to regard it as incidental that his average working day is from twelve to sixteen hours, depending on whether or not it is his turn to wake the residents at 6.30 a.m.

His work sometimes comes all at once when various people or

matters need attention, but there are other periods when little or nothing is going on. It is usually possible for him to have an hour or two off during the day.

Mr F. feels an active concern for the residents, but maintains that he does not become emotionally involved in the process. 'Leisure in the proper sense means the time that I am away from the building; it is to be regarded as a matter of geography,' he says. His off-duty days average eight a month. On these occasions he feels that he is able to extricate himself both physically and emotionally from his work ties. Apart from his enjoyment of music, his idea of leisure consists of meeting friends – none of whom is in social work – and going to the theatre and for long walks in the country.

*

Each one of these case studies is interesting for what it tells us about the lives of the people concerned, but collectively they are also of interest for what they can tell us about the similarities and differences of patterns of life. Some writers prefer to rely entirely on case studies in describing patterns of life. Thus Ronald Fraser, in introducing the first of two volumes on 'Work – Twenty Personal Accounts', criticizes the sociological approach which he thinks 'tends to turn people into objects'.[9] But he admits that 'the particular individual is always a part – indeed a product – of his society', and this points to the need for *some kind* of sociological analysis.

If the case studies are to amount to anything more than anecdotes we need to ask what is their sociological significance. Residential social workers are an extreme example of a category of people who are disposed, by the type of work they do and the circumstances in which they do it, to show a pattern of fusion of work and leisure. The demands of the job vary among each of the six individuals and so does their attitude to work and leisure. The case studies show how similar work situations in some ways induce a pattern of work and leisure shared by the group and in other ways allow differences in the way in which people play their occupational roles. The group pattern included the following variables:

Work situation

Workplace and living quarters are co-extensive
Work consists of helping people
Work tends to expand to fill the total time in residence

Work and leisure

Willingness to work during official time off
'Oases' of leisure in the working day
'Free time' equated with lack of responsibility for others

The individual differences in attitudes to work and leisure seen among the six people may be related to differences in their work situations. Mr A. and Mr F. represent two extremes and the following statements apply to Mr A., with those applying to Mr F. in parentheses:

Work situation

Workplace and living quarters highly (partly) co-extensive
Work consists of a variety (limited number) of ways of helping people
Work expands to fill the total time in residence almost completely (partly)

Work and leisure

Activities of work and leisure very similar (dissimilar)
Social contacts almost (not) entirely in the world of work
High (low) emotional involvement in the work
Caseworker role conceived as extensive (limited)

The other four people fall somewhere between these two extremes. The interviews suggest that, with each of the six, the more dissimilar they are in their work situation the more dissimilar they are in their pattern of work and leisure. In short, we may conclude that residential social workers as a group differ in their work and leisure patterns from other workers, but also differ among themselves in the extent to which they are physically and psychologically committed to their work.

(d) Local Government Councillors

We noted in Chapter 2 that the total space of non-work time is divisible for most people into 'pure' leisure (or freedom from obligations) and non-work obligations which they incur in meeting the necessities of life, in the service of their families or of other sections of the community. These non-work obligations may be placed on a scale of necessity-choice. Obligations to oneself by way of sleeping and eating have the minimum element of choice in them. Towards the middle of the scale are the obligations to one's family; these are conditioned by two types of choice – whether to assume responsibility for parents or other relatives, and whether to marry or have children. At the end of the scale where non-work obligations most closely resemble freely-chosen leisure pursuits come those activities which some people voluntarily perform in the service of groups outside their own families.

One of the many ways in which individuals may render public service is by being elected to their local council. No payment is given for the work, although councillors are entitled to claim for refund of expenses of various kinds. In many cases council and committee meetings take place in the evenings so that those in full-time employment may attend. Not only do councillors receive no pay for their public service; they also have to give up a considerable amount of their free time to perform it. Obviously they must gain some compensating satisfaction from this work.

A recent report made by the Government Social Survey to the Maud Committee on People in Local Government includes data which throw light on the role of council service in the lives of those who take part.[10] In addition to factual information from a sample of over 3,000 councillors and aldermen in England and Wales, interviews with a sub-sample of 598 were obtained and questions put on various aspects of council service and opinions on it. Although no questions were asked about councillors' leisure habits, the information they gave about the role of council work in their lives tells us something about the experience of 'work in leisure'.

An occupational difference was found in the amount of time spent on council work; manual workers spend about thirty per cent more, while small employers, managers and farmers (as a group) spend about twenty per cent less, than the average of 52 hours a month. Some of this difference is accounted for by the clustering of occupational groups in certain types of council: the fact that farmers are heavily over-represented on rural district councils, on which relatively little time is spent, helps to explain why the group that includes farmers puts in less time. But, even allowing for this, an occupational difference in spending time on council work still remains.

The survey provided data on why people take up council work, and the gains and losses involved. Informants were asked whether being a councillor had affected their private life. Younger councillors (under 45) more often said that their private lives had suffered and less often that they had been helped, and these proportions were reversed among older councillors (65 and over). However, an adverse effect on private life does *not* follow time spent on council work: the younger councillors spend rather less time on it than the older ones. Greater family responsibilities among younger councillors and the greater time available to the older and retired ones probably account for this.[11]

The various socio-economic groups were fairly evenly divided between those reporting adverse and favourable effects on private life, except that nearly twice as many manual workers said that it had suffered. The adverse effect on the private lives of socio-economic groups closely followed time spent on council work. It seems that the families of manual-worker councillors are less likely than the families of other types of councillor to accept without protest the inroads which council work makes into free time. Also, the fact that being a councillor less often helps the private lives of manual workers may mean that council experience has less relevance to their daily lives than it has for other types of councillor.

Informants were asked whether being a councillor had given them the opportunity of using abilities which they otherwise would not have used. The proportion saying that council work *had* given them such opportunities varied from fifty-two per cent of large employers, managers and professionals to eighty-two per cent of manual workers. There was also some difference in the *ways* in which potential abilities were felt to be used: the non-manual and manual worker groups were more likely than others to say that they had had opportunities for public speaking, widening their outlook and knowledge, and using organizing and administrative abilities. These are obviously the kind of abilities which few of them would be able to exercise in the course of their daily occupations.

A more detailed breakdown of the answers to the main question by particular socio-economic groups showed even wider differences. Thus one hundred per cent of the small group of foremen and supervisors said that council work had given them the opportunity of using potential abilities, compared with only thirty-three per cent among the self-employed professional workers. Clearly, the latter often have a working life which uses most of their abilities, whereas manual-worker councillors whose abilities have presumably led to their becoming foremen or supervisors may feel that their potential is even better used in council work.

The influence of council work in developing potential abilities is illustrated by what councillors said in answer to the question. The following are a selection of typical comments:

'It has brought a lot out in me – you surprise yourself that you're able to grasp so many details and so much knowledge of a wide variety of things.'

'If I didn't do this I would just be in a dead end job. It has sharpened my outlook and attitude – I understand people's problems better.'

'I am not an educated man but over the years I have been able to build up great confidence in myself. Thirty years ago I would never have dreamt of public speaking.'

Just under a third of the employed councillors interviewed found council work more satisfying than their daily occupation, a third preferred their occupation, and just over a third said they enjoyed both. More than half of the older councillors enjoyed both council work and occupation; council work was more often satisfying among the middle-aged councillors, and occupation most satisfying among the younger ones. Younger councillors tend more often than older ones to be in professional and intermediate non-manual occupations, including teaching, welfare work, etc. Some of these young councillors are at a stage in their occupational careers when they are just beginning to establish themselves, and perhaps also have the responsibilities of early married life. In these circumstances it would not be surprising if council work were to be seen as a kind of *supplement* to other aspects of life in general and to occupational life in particular.

Among middle-aged councillors council work becomes more often satisfying than occupation. During this period of life it may be that some individuals find that they have got as far as they can in their daily occupation, and turn to outside interests (for example, council work) for satisfaction and a sense of fresh achievement. If people do not find their occupation demanding or rewarding enough, they may well undertake council work for self-realization. Council work, then, may sometimes be a form of *compensation* for some kind of shortcoming felt in occupational life.

Councillors aged 65 and over appear to find occupation (when they still have one) and council work equally rewarding. At this age continuation in an occupation is likely to be voluntary. But twenty per cent of all councillors are retired, and for these, more than for employed councillors, public service must often become an important source of fulfilment and identity. For the retired we may say that council work is likely to be a *substitute* for a paid occupation. It is relevant to note that among aldermen (forty-eight per cent of whom are 65 or over) occupation is found more satisfying than council work by only twelve per cent.

So far it has been suggested that there are three types of relationship of council work to occupation: as supplement, as compensation and as substitute. A consideration of the attitudes of councillors in the various socio-economic groups helps to test this hypothesis. Only thirteen per cent of employers, managers, professionals and farmers found council work more satisfying than occupation, compared with sixty-four per cent of manual workers. It seems that whatever satisfactions most of the former group get from council work they are also able to get from their occupations. This would be consistent with their regarding council work as a supplement to occupation, at least in terms of providing personal satisfactions. For councillors whose jobs are more routine and offer less scope, however, council work is clearly often a means of obtaining satisfactions not offered by their occupations – their council work functions as compensation for the limitations of their daily jobs.

A more detailed breakdown of particular socio-economic groups shows even wider differences. Only one self-employed professional councillor (representing three per cent of his group) claimed to enjoy council work more than occupation, compared with seventy-four per cent among the semi-skilled manual workers. Also, the manual foremen and supervisors were closer to the non-manual and employer groups in their lesser preference for council work. It seems that the job of foreman or supervisor is likely to offer personal satisfactions closer to those of council work, and it is the ordinary manual-worker councillors who tend to find their major satisfactions outside their jobs and through council work.

Informants were asked whether being a councillor had affected their relations with people involved in their daily occupation. The employers, managers, professionals and farmers less often had work relations affected than had the non-manual and manual workers. The last two groups more often had work relations affected for the better *and* for the worse. The most frequent ways in which work relations were affected for the better were that informants felt they were more respected by colleagues and that their circle was extended. Typical comments illustrating this kind of answer were:

'I have rather more prestige – the managers of my firm respect me, too.'

'Becoming a councillor affected recognition in my country – I was promoted soon afterwards.'

The most frequent ways in which work relations were affected for the worse were that business was lost, people were offended, or work relations were made more difficult. Thus:

'You need a lot of time off – this affects one's colleagues and they tend to view you as a bit of a nuisance – especially your immediate superiors.'

'I have to meet 250 people per week – they often ask me to help and when I can't I lose business because they don't buy through me any more.'

A measure of general satisfaction with council work is the frequency of giving it up or wanting to give it up. The rank order of turnover of socio-economic groups on councils is the same as the rank order of proportions intending to give it up after a while or in the near future – the large employers, managers and professionals highest and the manual workers lowest. Professional and self-employed councillors have a turnover rate more than fifty per cent above the average. Only one per cent of manual workers intended to give up council work soon, compared with twelve to fourteen per cent in the other socio-economic groups.

It seems reasonable to conclude that council work fulfils characteristically different functions in the lives of people in the various occupational groups. The fact that proportionately more employers, managers and professionals are councillors than are those in other occupations indicates that the qualifications needed for these employments, and the experience gained in them, are similar to those of council work. The method of recruitment is obviously a factor in determining the kind of people who join councils, but the political parties and other sponsoring agencies can only bring in those who can be persuaded to stand.[12] Relatively few manual workers have so far been persuaded to stand or have put themselves forward for election, and the present manual-workers councillors are probably very unrepresentative in many ways of manual workers generally.

It has been noted that when manual workers *are* brought into council work they appear to get much more involved in it than do other types of councillors – they spend more time on it, their private lives more often suffer because of it, they more often use potential abilities in it, and they less often want to give it up. For many of them, council service seems to have the strong motive of *compensation* for shortcomings felt in occupational life. To a lesser extent, this also seems to be true of the non-manual worker group. The relation between occupation and council work for this type of councillor may be called one of *opposition*.

The content of, and types of, social relationship involved in his daily occupation and his council work are usually very different. He more often has difficulty with both his family and his work relations because council work is in a sense an alien experience – and probably it is often not 'expected of him'.

Rather different factors enter into the motivation of employers, managers and professionals to become councillors. The kind of work they do for a living – dealing with people, studying documents, making administrative or policy decisions – has much in common with their work as councillors. Their occupational obligations may well intrude into time which could be given to council work, and not surprisingly they spend less than the average time on it. In the case of self-employed professionals, not only do they fail to feel a sense of using potential abilities in council work; they also have a greater tendency to give it up. This all adds up to a weaker motivation to serve on councils – one of *supplementing* a fairly full and self-expressive working life. They may share with manual worker councillors the motive of public service, but they do not have such a personal *need* for council work and the satisfactions it can bring. In terms of work and leisure, council work is an *extension* of their occupational life. This extension pattern would also apply to many retired councillors, in that council work is to some extent a substitute for the interest and involvement they had in their occupations.

Differences between the extension and opposition patterns lie partly in occupational experience and also in council experience. If those whose occupations involve administrative work or making policy decisions find their major satisfaction (or at least, sense of social usefulness) in this aspect of council work then there is some continuity between the two roles. On the other hand, much council work consists of dealing with the problems of individuals, and neither this nor policy making may have much in common with the occupational experiences of most manual-worker councillors.

Being a rural district councillor is not such an onerous business as being a county borough councillor. Farmer employers and managers account for thirty per cent of rural district councillors, and these may be seen as a third group in terms of the relation between occupation and council work. They put in less time as councillors and more often prefer their occupation to council work, but they do feel they use potential abilities as councillors and they do tend to remain longer than do other types. They experience less of the competition between occupation and council work that many of those with the extension pattern do. Instead, they seem to have worked out a middling pattern of *neutrality* between occupation and council work, which may help to explain why proportionately so many councillors are farmer employers or managers.

Most of the above analysis has been concerned with the relation between council work and occupation. Council work is one kind of non-work obligation, and whether such obligations are undertaken depends to some extent on the willingness to forgo leisure pursuits. Unfortunately no questions were asked in the survey about councillors' leisure, and so it is not possible to present any evidence concerning the possible interrelationship between occupation, council work and leisure. We do, however, know that councillors spend on average about twelve hours a week on their public duties, and some spend substantially more than this. For them, as for the residential social workers discussed in the previous section, leisure of the conventional type must be very scarce and sometimes even non-existent. It seems likely that councillors are generally recruited from that section of the population whose leisure needs are low. Perhaps it is not uncharitable to suggest that councillors are sometimes able to find leisure-like experiences and satisfactions in the course of performing their public duties.

8 Towards a Theory of Work-Leisure Relationships

There are broadly two schools of thought about the relation of spheres of life in our present type of urban-industrial society. The first – whose adherents may be called segmentalists – hold that people's lives are split into different areas of activity and interest, with each social segment lived out more or less independently of the rest. Work, they say, is separated from leisure, production from consumption, workplace from residence, education from religion, politics from recreation. The second school – the holists – maintain that society is essentially an integrated whole, every part of which affects and is affected to some degree, by every other part. Attitudes and practices developed in one sphere of life, they say, can spill over into another – killing time at work can become killing time in leisure, apathy in the workplace can become apathy in politics, alienation from the one, alienation from the other.

These holist and segmentalist schools of thought about society as a whole may be related to the arguments of the supporters of fusion or polarity as explanations of trends in the relationship between work and leisure. The evidence for fusion and polarity was considered in Chapter 6 and found to be inconclusive when considering society as a whole. With holism and segmantalism, however, it is not so much a matter of weighing up evidence as of accepting or rejecting a philosophy of life.

Each of us *has* a philosophy of life, whether or not we consciously think about it. In considering the ways in which work and leisure pose problems for us in our own lives we tend to adopt one outlook rather than another. The sort of solutions we prescribe for ourselves or for other people stem from the particular philosophy we hold. Whether these prescribed solutions 'work', whether they can be put into practice, depends on how closely they fit the conditions of our society. The conditions of society include, of course, other men's ideas and philosophies. It makes a difference to each of us how the others think, especially since it is becoming harder and harder to 'contract out' of society. This is not to say that we should all be conformists, but it does mean that the most successful rebels challenge the existing order of things from *within* society, not by withdrawing from it.

The alternative philosophies of holism and segmentalism have implications for the integration of the individual in society. With the segmentalist view, the individual may be seen as forced to pick and choose, to divide his loyalties, and to become what McClung Lee has called 'multivalent man' – changing his social self to fit in with the values of the groups he belongs to as he moves from one to another.[1] With the holist view, the essential unity of society and of culture is seen as leading to a decline in the creative autonomy of the individual, a general sense of oppression, and a feeling that there is no escape from the total pattern of life to which we find ourselves committed. Both views appear to be valid to some extent when we consider society as a whole, and the problem when we consider smaller groups or individuals is to determine when work and leisure can be experienced as separate and often opposed spheres, and when the character of the one sphere spills over into the other. If we assume that work, in its most creative forms, fulfils certain human needs, we may ask what happens to these needs when the quality of working life is too poor to fulfil them. Most jobs today are regarded by the mass of people as only a means to the end of earning a living. Jobs are generally not a source of *positive* satisfaction – the fact that in surveys most people say they are 'satisfied' with their jobs simply means that they expect very little from them or that they can find no better job. In most cases the worker finds his real sense of satisfaction after he leaves the workplace. This does not necessarily mean that satisfaction is found outside work itself, defined in wider terms than paid employment. For some people the need for creative expression of workmanship flourishes in leisure, in do-it-yourself work, the care of cars or gardens, the 'inventive puttering of life after work'.[2]

Levels and Patterns

There are two levels on which we may consider the various possible types of relationship between work and leisure: in the life of the individual and in the structure of the society in which he lives. This, in fact, oversimplifies the matter because there are levels intermediate between the individual and the societal (such as the group), but the analysis should be clearer if confined to these two levels and to a general description of the type of relationship (Fig. 1).

Fig. 1 Types of Work–Leisure Relationship

General description	Individual level	Societal level
identity	extension	fusion
contrast	opposition	polarity
separateness	neutrality	containment

The general descriptions are the broadest possible ways in which we can look at work and leisure, covering both individuals and the society of which they are part. *Identity* describes any situation where work and leisure feature similar structures, behaviour or purposes. *Contrast* means a definition of the content of one sphere as the absence or opposite of the other. *Separateness* sums up a situation of minimal contact or influence between the spheres. It will be helpful to remember these general descriptions when considering the different types of relationship between work and leisure and the important question of whether there is a connection between the two levels.

Let us first discuss the proposition that there are three types of relationship between work and leisure and that each of us tends to have one of these in his own pattern of life. We introduced in the previous chapter the terms 'extension', 'opposition' and 'neutrality' to describe the various types of relationship between occupation and council work for local government councillors. Now we can see how far these terms may be used to group together the patterns of work and leisure shown by the other types of people mentioned.

Briefly, the *extension* pattern consists of having leisure activities which are often similar in content to one's working activities and of making no sharp distinction between what is considered as work and what as leisure. With the *opposition* pattern leisure activities are deliberately unlike work and there is a sharp distinction between what is work and what is leisure. Finally, the *neutrality* pattern consists of having leisure activities which are generally different from work but not deliberately so, and of appreciating the difference between work and leisure without always defining the one as the absence of the other.

Before going on to examine these individual patterns of work–leisure relationship in detail, we should look briefly at their equivalents at the societal level. Extension of work into leisure (and vice versa) in the life of the person is paralleled by fusion of work and leisure spheres in the society as a whole. Individual opposition of work and leisure is matched by polarity of the spheres in society. Individual neutrality between work and leisure is matched by containment of the spheres in society. This is not to say that the societal arrangements for work and leisure necessarily impose themselves on every aspect of our personal lives. But it is obviously easier to sustain a personal pattern that is in line with the pattern of society, or at least of that part of society in which we move. For example, if we want to keep work and leisure as distinctly opposite parts of our life we shall find this easier to do in a society that keeps places of work free from the influence of leisure and places of leisure free from the taint of work.

Returning to work–leisure relationships at the individual level, these first need carefully defining. Then we may look at the aspects of occupations and work involvement ('work variables') that seem to be associated with each of these patterns of relationship. Finally, we deal with the non-work (mainly leisure) variables that are also associated with the patterns. In this way we build up a total picture of what it means to have an extension, opposition or neutrality pattern of work and leisure.

In Fig. 2 all the details are set out in summary form. The various descriptions or values of the variables are based on research conclusions already noted in earlier chapters, but sometimes a certain amount of speculation is involved. Further research may require that some of the details be changed or qualified.

Work-leisure relationship variables	Extension	Opposition	Neutrality
Content of work and leisure	similar	deliberately different	usually different
Demarcation of spheres	weak	strong	average
Central life interest	work	—	non-work
Imprint left by work on leisure	marked	marked	not marked

Work variables			
Autonomy in work situation	high	—	low
Use of abilities (how far extended)	fully ('stretched')	unevenly ('damaged')	not ('bored')
Involvement	moral	alienative	calculative
Work colleagues	include some close friends	—	include no close friends
Work encroachment on leisure	high	low	low
Typical occupations	social workers (especially residential)	'extreme' (mining fishing)	routine clerical and manual

Non-work variables			
Educational level	high	low	medium
Duration of leisure	short	irregular	long
Main function of leisure	continuation of personal development	recuperation	entertainment

To put some flesh on the bare bones of Fig. 2 we may consider just what it means in human terms to have each of these patterns. With the extension pattern there is a similarity between at least some work and leisure activities and a lack of demarcation made between what is called work and what is called leisure. The extreme cases of people having this pattern are those mentioned in Chapter 2 who are free from the necessity of earning a living but who do work of a kind and in circumstances they choose. A larger group of people are those whose lives show a strong *tendency* to extension of work into leisure but also some elements of opposition and/or neutrality. Thus some social workers feel that it is bad for them and for their clients if they are too work-dominated, and their leisure accordingly has some elements of deliberate opposition to work. Having work as a central life interest is part of the definition of the extension pattern. This is because work to someone who sees a continuity between work and leisure is a much more embracing concept than just 'the job' or even 'the occupation'. Work signifies the meaning and fulfilment of life, and in saying that it is also the *centre* of life such people are not necessarily denying the integrated role that leisure plays in it. Also, because of deep involvement in their kind of work it leaves a relatively great imprint on the rest of their lives – it is often an influence from which they are never really free.

The key aspects of the opposition pattern are the intentional dissimilarity of work and leisure and the strong demarcation between the two spheres. The extreme cases of this pattern are those who hate their work so much that any reminder of it in their off-duty time is unpleasant. But paradoxically such people do not in one sense get away from work at all: so deeply are they marked by the hated experience of work that they measure the delights of leisure according to how much unlike work they are. Thus if work means submission to authority then leisure means 'having a go' at authority in some other way. A less pure type of opposition between work and leisure is shown by the person who has an ambivalent rather than a completely hostile attitude to work – he hates it because of the physical or psychological damage that he feels it does to him, yet he 'loves' it because he is fascinated by its arduousness or by its dangers (it is 'real man's work'). The strain of such work ensures that it is not carried over into leisure, from which it is clearly demarcated. The source of central life interest in cases of opposition is generally not clear; if work is viewed with unmixed hatred then presumably non-work is seen as the centre of life, but if there is a love-hate relationship to work then either sphere could be seen as central, or perhaps the very opposition and dissimilarity of the spheres renders the person incapable of making a comparative judgment.

The third pattern of neutrality is only partly defined by a

'usually different' content of work and leisure and by an 'average' demarcation of spheres. This pattern is *not* intermediate between the extension and opposition patterns, although it may at first glance appear to be so. The crucial difference between extension and opposition on the one hand and neutrality on the other is that the former denote respectively a positive and negative *attachment* to work, while the latter denotes a *detachment* from work that is, in Berger's phase, neither fulfilment nor oppression.[3] In the cases of extension and opposition, the imprint left by work on leisure is relatively marked, in either a positive or a negative way. But people showing the neutrality pattern are neither so engrossed in their work that they want to carry it over into non-work time nor so damaged by it that they develop a hostile or love-hate relation to it. Instead, work leaves them comparatively unmarked and free to carry over into leisure the non-involvement and passivity which characterizes their attitude to work. In other words, detachment from any real responsibility for and interest in work leads to detachment from any active and constructive leisure pursuits. Although some individuals are able to break out of this vicious circle, the tendency is to sit back and wait to be entertained. Since entertainment is more 'fun' than work, people with the neutrality pattern are likely to find their central life interest outside the work sphere.

Associated Variables

Turning now to the work variables associated with the three patterns we may note first the effect of degree of autonomy in the work situation. The study of social workers with relatively high autonomy showed that they were also very likely to exhibit the extension pattern. On the other hand, the bank workers, who generally had little autonomy, typically showed the neutrality pattern. The conclusion regarding the opposition pattern is not so clear. Probably autonomy is low for most of these people, being accompanied by little interest in the work itself and hence a desire to escape from it. But a highly individualistic work situation, neither machine-paced nor closely supervised, could also be accompanied by opposition of work and leisure if the *attitude* to work were one of alienation.

The second work variable, use of abilities, needs to be analysed both in terms of amount and evenness of being extended or 'used' in the job. The social workers, who used most of their abilities in an intensive way, tended to show the extension pattern, while the bank workers, who were less extended in their jobs, tended to show the neutrality pattern. Those who are unevenly extended in their jobs are likely to want to compensate for this by a counterbalancing type of non-work life that will help to repair the ravages of work. To sum this up we can say that extension is usually accompanied by a feeling of being 'stretched' by the work, neutrality by being 'bored' with it, and opposition by being 'damaged' by it.

To describe types of involvement in work we may draw upon Amitai Etzioni's types of involvement by 'lower participants' in organizations – moral, calculative and alienative.[4] Since we are restricting our analysis to economic (employing) organizations and do not, as Etzioni does, include a comparison of economic with other kinds of organization, the parallel is not an exact one; it may nevertheless be worth making. Accepting that economic reward is a common motive for employees to participate in work organizations, we may describe as 'moral' the kind of involvement which would produce a desire to go on working in that way even if freed from the necessity of earning a living. 'Calculative' involvement would occur where the work was done consciously as part of a transaction, that is, where economic reward was overwhelmingly the main motivation. 'Alienative' involvement would occur where the economic reward was also important but was experienced less as a transaction than as a sense of being forced to do the job against one's will. These three types of involvement seem to be associated respectively with the extension, neutrality and opposition patterns of work and leisure, although there is a certain amount of ambiguity between the last two patterns.

The likelihood of having some work colleagues among one's close friends is high among those with the extension pattern and low among those with the neutrality pattern. Again, the opposition pattern is not clear in this respect. If work is hated then presumably the thought of mixing with work colleagues off the job is also hateful, and this may help to explain the feeling among some factory workers that 'mating is not palling'. But it is also possible that the damaging experience of work is made more tolerable by the feeling of solidarity with workmates whose company may well be sought off the job. An 'occupational community' does not require that all members be *positively* involved in the work: all may be *negatively* involved, provided that they are conscious of sharing this feeling.

The degree of encroachment of work on leisure is high for those with the extension pattern and low for the other two groups. The 'extension' people are likely to let their work carry over into leisure time because they find it interesting for its own sake. Where work does encroach on the leisure time of the 'neutrality' group, it is likely to do so only as a means to an end, for example, to pass examinations in order to get promotion. Where work encroaches on the leisure time of the 'opposition' group, it does so only in the sense that a man must first recover from the effects of this kind of work before he can enjoy leisure.

The above analysis of work variables in relation to types of work–leisure relationship has been based on the research reported in earlier chapters. This research has mostly been concerned with specific occupational groups, although the effects of certain variables *within* occupational groups have also been noted. It is not claimed that certain occupations and certain types of work–leisure relationship always go together, but to round off the discussion of work variables the following tentative additions may be made to the typical occupations listed in Fig. 2. Extension: successful businessmen (perhaps they *are* successful because they have little or no time for leisure), doctors, teachers and craft workers. Neutrality: minor professionals other than social workers. Opposition: unskilled manual workers, assembly-line workers, oil rig workers, tunnellers (the last two being 'extreme' occupations in the sense both of high pay and physical working conditions).

We now come to three non-work variables – one of education and two of leisure. Concerning education, the child care officers, a majority of whom showed the extension pattern, also had a majority who had attended university. The bank employees, a majority of whom showed the neutrality pattern, had mostly attended grammar schools but had not gone on to further education. A large majority of the 'opposition' manual workers had had only elementary or secondary modern last full-time education. The question arises: is it type of education that determines the occupation that in turn determines work–leisure patterns, or does education exert an influence on work–leisure patterns independently of occupation? There are two clues to the answer to this difficult question. One is my own impression gained from the pilot interviews with business and service workers. Several of the people in business occupations who had a neutrality work–leisure pattern had been well educated (university or public school) yet seemed far less involved in their work than some of the less well educated social workers who had an extension pattern. Secondly, the analysis of the attitudes of local government councillors showed that a number of manual-worker councillors had been so 'educated' by their experience of public work that they now felt capable of doing things which they earlier felt they would have been precluded from doing by their low level of formal education. Both of these clues point in the direction of the influence of work experience on work–leisure patterns independently of the level of formal education.

There is ample evidence that professional and business employees have less leisure time than the mass of routine clerical and manual workers.[5] This suggests 'short' and 'long' duration of leisure time for those showing the extension and neutrality patterns respectively. Again, the opposition pattern presents problems. The distant-water fishermen have about nine months of the year at sea and three months ashore, mostly as leisure time; the latter, therefore, is better described as 'irregular' rather than as either long or short. In the case of others with the opposition pattern, the lack of work encroachment on leisure may mean a relatively long duration of leisure, but a willingness to work long hours for big money would shorten available leisure time. There is, then, no general conclusion about duration of leisure time for those with the opposition pattern.

Finally, there is the question of the main function of leisure. Here it seems reasonable to borrow and slightly modify Dumazedier's functions of personal development, entertainment and relaxation to apply to extension, neutrality and opposition respectively.[6] For 'personal development' we may substitute *continuation of personal development*, since the work done by people with the extension pattern is usually capable of initiating personal development and the need is for leisure to continue it in a different or complementary way. *Entertainment* has the right connotation of relief from boredom to describe the function of 'neutrality' leisure. 'Relaxation', on the other hand, is too similar to, and implies too much of the passivity of, entertainment to describe 'opposition' leisure, and the term *recuperation*, which could include the explosive compensatory function of leisure noted by Wilensky,[7] seems preferable. It should be realized that only in exceptional cases does any one of these three functions characterize the whole of leisure. For example, we may say that a person has the extension pattern because the *general* nature of the relationship between his work and his leisure is as outlined in Fig. 2, but that need not stop him from sometimes feeling the need for recuperation or for entertainment.

It now remains to relate what was said earlier in this chapter about the philosophies of segmentalism and holism to the general (individual and societal) types of work–leisure relationship. This means that we can try to see a connection between how people think about the world (society and themselves), how the societal spheres of work and leisure are related, and how the work and leisure parts of their lives are related. The suggested parallels are set out in Fig. 3.

Fig. 3 The Connection Between Philosophies and
Work–Leisure Relationships

Philosophy	Work–Leisure Relationship
Holism	Identity
Segmentalism	{ Contrast { Separateness

A person who sees that the parts of his life are integrated, each one affecting and being affected by the others (holism), is likely to have an extension pattern of work and leisure and to live in a society – or at least in a social circle – in which the spheres of work and leisure are fused (identity). On the other hand, a person who sees the parts of his life as separate segments comparatively unaffected by each other (segmentalism) is likely to have either of the other two types of work–leisure relationships. Either he will have an opposition pattern of work and leisure and live in a society of polarized work–leisure relationships *or* he will have a neutrality pattern of work and leisure and live in a society in which work and leisure are fairly self-contained.

The above explanations and suggestions are not a mere academic exercise. They are intended to show how philosophy (or 'world view'), society and individual are linked. If we are interested in the relationship between work and leisure at one of these levels, to understand it fully we must consider how it is reinforced at the other levels. To ask which is the better individual pattern of work and leisure is also to ask which is the better societal organization of work and leisure and which is the better philosophy regarding them. To be able to make changes on any one of these levels we must concern ourselves with what implications these changes have for the other levels. Failure to do so will probably mean that no worthwhile change will be achieved.

9 The Potentialities of Work and Leisure

In these final two chapters our main concern will be to see how the type of philosophy and social structure affect individual work–leisure relationships, both as they are and as they could be. In this chapter the possibility that there are broad types of person with respect to seeking fulfilment in either work or leisure will first be considered. Then the way in which work and leisure spheres confront each other in contemporary industrial society will be posed as a problem, to which it will be suggested there are two main kinds of answer: the *differentiation* or the *integration* of work and leisure. Finally, these alternatives will be discussed in the light of their potentialities to fulfil human needs.

Types of Person

Studies of different work situations and of individual involvement in work clearly show the wide variation in the content and conditions of work in modern industrial societies and the range of involvement from almost complete identification to almost complete estrangement or alienation. The question arises: to what extent are there different types of *person* with respect to having needs to be satisfied mainly in work or in leisure, as well as different types of work situation and work involvement? The question is asked mainly by psychologists, whose special interest is *individual* behaviour, but it also has relevance for sociologists, whose special interest is *socially patterned* behaviour. Let us approach this problem by quoting the views of a psychologist (John Fraser) who is concerned with the philosophical question of the meaning that work ought to have in a person's life:

Ought [the individual] to find in [work] his principal means of self-expression? Ought it to be the cause of his deepest satisfactions? Should it be the biggest thing in his life? This is to demand a great deal both of the individual and the job, and it is unlikely that more than a small proportion of any community will ever approach such a standard. Nor may it be desirable that they should, for the number of individuals who have this level of motivation to pour into their work is limited, while the number of jobs into which it would be worth pouring it is similarly restricted. On the other hand, ought work to make as few demands as possible on the individual? Ought it to offer only a limited sense of achievement or identification? Ought it to become a means of putting in part of the day quite agreeably while at the same time providing the wherewithal to finance his home and leisure pursuits? There are individuals to whom a job like this would make a strong appeal and who might find their real satisfactions in others areas of their life. Between these extremes there will be jobs and individuals with different levels of expectation and satisfaction to offer and receive, and if we were to match up each with the other we might claim to have achieved the ideal industrial community. Those who expected a great deal from their work and were prepared to put a lot into it would be in jobs which utilized all their potentialities to the full and gave them in return a deep sense of personal achievement. Those who neither expected nor were prepared to contribute very much would be in the comfortable, undemanding jobs where they would be reasonably occupied, well paid and contented.[1]

There is a curious mixture of narrowness and breadth of vision in Fraser's remarks. He raises the *prescriptive* question of the place of work in human life, and at the beginning appears to be discussing the potentialities of man in general rather than of men of a particular time and place. Yet this statements about the proportion of men with high work motivation and 'the number of jobs into which it would be worth pouring it' are largely *descriptive*. He appears to be treating the level of work motivation as something which is entirely a personal characteristic of individuals, independent of the kind of work which may be open to them and unaffected by their experience of work which has the potentiality for changing the attitudes of those who do it. It is true that, by the standards of those whose work has reasonable scope for personal involvement, there are relatively few jobs today which reach these standards. However, there is nothing immutable about the proportion of jobs which people may regard as 'worthy' of personal involvement. The criteria of estimation of worth may change, but so may the content and conditions of the jobs. Whether the latter happens or not is largely a matter of whether enough people agitate for changes which would make their work a more rewarding personal experience.

The idea of matching levels of personal work involvement to levels of objectively 'involving' work is superficially attractive, but assumes both personal attitudes and occupational structures to be constants. It is true that we know very little about the relative contributions of initial personal preferences and subsequent work experiences in shaping present work values. It is very difficult, for example, to say to what extent social workers tend to be highly work-involved because of the nature of the work they do or because, being the sort of people they are, they were led to seek highly demanding work. But we certainly should not ignore the feedback effect that work experiences can have on the values and motivations with which people enter occupations. There was some evidence of this in the pilot interviews with older informants in business and service occupations; a few of them could recall their early feelings about the work they entered, and how different these were from the pattern of adjustment to circumstances they had subsequently worked out. Thus one insurance manager, having started out in the business world many years ago with a good education and high hopes, somewhat sadly remarked that 'your abilities and potentialities tend to equate themselves with the work you do.'

If we were to adopt the 'matching' idea suggested by Fraser we should need to be quite clear about what we were matching with what. Presumably the matching would not be done until at least after school-leaving age. But already certain differences in attitude to work would have emerged which could not be attributed wholly to differences in personality type. Assuming the present structure of family life and education, some children would have been brought up in a home and school environment that would encourage them to seek interest and a sense of achievement from work, while others would expect little from work and therefore feel 'satisfied' with low-level occupations. The occupational structure, too, would be regarded as given. Jobs which presumably would be regarded as unsuitable for those with high work involvement would be offered to those who 'neither expected nor were prepared to contribute very much', as a result of which the latter would never know how much they might be prepared to contribute if they were placed in a work environment that encouraged contribution.

To adapt a Marxist phrase used in connexion with society as a whole to the sphere of work and leisure, it scarcely seems an exaggeration to say that there are 'two classes in society': the privileged with respect to a unified and fulfilling work–leisure life, and the underprivileged. As Henry Durant remarked, for some men and women the problem of leisure does not arise:

They all obtain satisfaction from their work. All of them have some sphere of independent action, or they are presented with problems and difficulties with which they must grapple and solve; none of them are automata. . . . Because of this, and because, finding satisfaction in their work, they do not desire to flee from it as soon as the immediate job is completed, the impact of their profession or work is clearly discernible in all their activities. There is for them no sharp break. They read books which have relevance to their job; similarly they attend lectures and follow courses of study; they move predominantly amongst people who have the same interests and so discuss the problems of their daily task while they are not actually dealing with them. . . . In short the method of earning their livelihood determines for them their mode of living. And it does this in such a way that they obtain satisfaction. Hence they need not search for compensations in other directions; they do not require soporifics from the world of amusement . . . they will tend to bring to such aspects of their lives the same attitude and qualities of mind as are required and developed by their work.[2]

My research confirms that there is a group of people who tend to have such a work–leisure pattern, and that there are two other groups who differ from it but who for the present purpose may be considered as one. In this book the major concern has been to establish that certain *associations* between work and leisure variables exist. without necessarily implying a *causal* relationship. My view is that the causal influence is more likely to be *from* work experiences and attitudes *to* leisure experiences and attitudes than the other way round, mainly because the work sphere is both more structured and more basic to life itself, though it may be conceded that there is something to say for Tom Burns's proposition that there 'is a tendency for the organising principles of leisure to extend into work life.'[3] But which is cause and which is effect is not crucial to the description of the quality of the relationship. In terms of individuals, the point is that some men in the past have led, and some today do lead 'unitary lives in which the excellence obtainable during leisure characterizes the work in which they engage,'[4] while others – the underprivileged – have 'excellence' in neither sphere. The question arises: to what extent is this distribution of excellence the inevitable product of personality differences rooted in human nature, or the potentially changeable product of a particular type of social structure which distributes the 'means to excellence' unevenly?

A full answer to this question would require research beyond any that has so far been carried out. Ideally it would require a long-term research project so that certain types of personality could be identified *before* they entered the world of work and could then be followed up to see to what extent their subsequent work and leisure behaviour and attitudes corresponded to a predicted pattern. In the absence of such research, we should keep an open mind about the relative effects of 'nature' and 'nurture' in this respect.

Problem: The Confrontation of Work and Leisure

The quality of the work and leisure lives of the mass of people in a society becomes a problem when the confrontation of the two spheres reveals shortcomings in either or both, or when a minority appears to have achieved conditions and satisfactions which give the majority a sense of relative deprivation. The view that there are two kinds of person with respect to seeking fulfilment in either work or leisure does not avoid perceiving a problem, but it makes that problem a fairly narrow one: how to adjust kinds of person to kinds of potentially fulfilling situations within something like the present division of labour and leisure. But if we reject the view that there are two such kinds of person, the problem becomes much wider: what kind of social structure is necessary to give *all* people opportunities for fulfilment in work *and* leisure, and how can various individual needs be reconciled with the 'needs' of society itself? To implement this could involve a radically new division of labour and leisure. The policy aspect of these questions will be dealt with in the next chapter, but before that it may be helpful to seek to clarify the ways in which the confrontation of work and leisure poses problems for contemporary industrial society, and the possible ways in which these problems may be resolved.

In pre-industrial societies there was no confrontation between work and leisure because work itself contained such leisure-like activities as society could afford its members. At the height of the Industrial Revolution work, which had been purged of much of its leisure content by the Protestant ethic for the middle classes and by factory work subsistence wage levels for the working class, confronted a leisure scarcely worth the name. It is only in the modern phase of industrialism, with the shorter working week and greater purchasing power of the masses, that leisure has become a significant sphere of life. But, as we have shown, there are the privileged and the underprivileged with respect to re-warding work and leisure experiences. Assuming that these differences cannot be explained wholly in terms of differences in personality type, there is the question of what to do about the underprivileged. To put the problem simply: a large number of people today have work and leisure lives which are neither satisfying nor creative. What should be done?

A number of detailed answers are possible, but they may be grouped into two general types: those which stem from the two philosophies of segmentalism and holism. The guiding principles of these answers are respectively *differentiation* and *integration* and they will be considered in turn.

Answer 1: The Differentiation of Work and Leisure

Those who advocate the differentiation of work and leisure as the solution to at least some of the problems in either sphere do so on the assumption, explicit or implicit, that the segmentation of spheres is a characteristic and desirable feature of modern industrial society. Robert Dubin puts this point of view as follows:

... I assume that modern urban-industrial life is highly segmented, and that at a behavioural level this is its very central feature. All of what we mean by secularization of life, by freedom, and by privacy derives from this segmented and compartmented way in which modern life is lived out. Indeed, I would be constrained to argue that the rate of innovation and the radicalness of innovations in all realms of modern living (from the arts, through science and technology, through social relations to morals and values) can be traced directly to the segmentation of the realms of life. I would go further and argue that the adjustment of individual to society is enhanced on a probabilistic basis, for there are now manifestly many more niches into which any individual can 'fit' and among which he may choose insofar as personal choice is a factor in finding a place in the modern community.[5]

There are two distinct ideas in what Dubin is saying here: the *understanding* that society is segmented and the *belief* that the perceived segmentation encourages innovation and the adjustment of individuals to society. As applied to work and leisure, the first proposition relates to the 'polarity' hypothesis, evidence for and against which was reviewed in Chapter 6. Here we are mainly concerned with the second proposition in that it relates to the realization of social and individual potentialities. There can be little quarrel with the part of the proposition concerning innovation in all realms of modern life. Segmentation – including *differentiation* of structure and function and manifest in such features as the division of labour and complex organizations – is unquestionably a characteristic of the development of modern industrial society. The controversial point concerns the adjustment of the individual to society. The model of society implicit in the statement that 'there are now manifestly many more niches into which any given individual can "fit"' is one in which such fitting or not fitting is the result of a transaction between the individual and society. It is the task of society, this argument runs, not to impose a pattern of social relationships on the individual but to offer him a set of alternatives. Dubin is in effect arguing that a society in which failure to 'adjust' in one sphere means failure to 'adjust' in *all* spheres is less desirable than a society in which failure is compartmented and therefore restricted. Most people would agree that it is better to have a choice of opportunities to adjust than a compulsion to adjust to a totalitarian society. But we must beware of imagining that the life spheres of individuals and the institutions of modern industrial societies are more autonomous than they actually are. It may sound a superficially attractive solution to say, 'If our work doesn't offer us a chance to think and be creative we must compensate for this in leisure.' However, as we shall see, there must be considerable doubt about the quality of the 'success' obtainable in one isolated sphere.

Georges Friedmann is one of the best-known exponents of the doctrine of the differentiation of work and leisure as the answer to problems in both spheres. He does not in the long run abandon the task of 'humanizing' work, as some others do, and so his views represent the case for differentiation in perhaps its strongest form. 'First, there must be a revaluation of work, which, to be complete, must be carried out simultaneously on three different planes, intellectual, social and moral. Secondly, there must be opportunities for self-realization and self-development for the individual in non-work activities.'[6] He sees greater progress being made towards the latter goal, since '. . . there are still today millions of jobs which cannot be revalued in such ways, and this will continue to be the case for a long while yet.'[7] His pessimism about the possibility of work revaluation makes him write, in connection with the reduction of working hours resulting from automation, of 'the need to find a new *centre* for human development in the hours thus freed, i.e. in the active use of leisure . . .'[8] (my emphasis).

The trouble with Friedmann's views is that they appear to be advocating changes in both work and leisure spheres but in fact the key to the whole problem is seen as leisure. Making leisure 'a new centre' is something we can do fairly easily, he implies, while the reorganization of work is much more difficult. Two things have to be done, the one short-term and relatively easy to accomplish, the other long-term and much more difficult. Let us, he argues, tackle the easier part of the programme first. Unfortunately, this outlook usually means that the more difficult part of the programme is deferred indefinitely. Moreover, the victories that are gained in one field are nullified if the campaign is never started in the other. From time to time people who have been deprived in both their work and leisure lives are given the opportunity, through a large football pools win, of making leisure the centre of their lives. On the whole they do not make a success of this, and there is no reason to suppose that a society that seeks to make leisure the 'centre for human development', while leaving the problem of work untackled, will succeed any better.

Another French writer, Jacques Ellul, challenges Friedmann's views:

... Friedmann writes 'We must conjure up the prospect of a society in which labour will be of restricted duration, industrial operations automatized, and piecework, requiring no attention, made pleasant by music and lectures ... a society, in short, in which culture will be identified completely with leisure. In a leisure more and more full of potentialities, and more and more active, will be found the justification of the humanistic experiment.'

Friedmann is asserting here that it is impossible to make industrial labour positive. But if we agree to Friedmann's proposition that the human being can develop his personality only in the cultivation of leisure, we are denying that work is an element of personality fulfilment, or of satisfaction, or of happiness. This is bad enough; but the situation is even more serious when we consider that putting our hopes in leisure is really taking refuge in idealism. If leisure were a real vacuum, a break with the forces of the environment, and if, moreover, it were spontaneously utilized for the education of the personality, the thesis of the value of leisure might hold. But neither of these conditions is true.

We see first of all that leisure, instead of being a vacuum representing a break with society, is literally stuffed with technical mechanisms of compensation and integration ... Leisure time is a mechanized time and is exploited by techniques which, although different from those of man's ordinary work, are as invasive, exacting, and leave man no more free than labour itself. As to the second condition, it is simply not the case that the individual, left on his own, will devote himself to the education of his personality or to a spiritual and cultural life ...

We conclude that the education of the human personality cannot but conform to the postulates of technical civilization. Man's leisure must reinforce the other elements of this culture so that there will be no risk of producing poorly adjusted persons. This is the direction the techniques of amusement have taken. To gamble that leisure will enable man to live is to sanction the dissociation I have been describing and to cut him off completely from a part of life.[9]

Ellul's language is impassioned, but what he says is more in line with such facts as we have about the relationship between work and leisure than the apparently more practical, but in fact more idealistic, position of Friedmann. The confrontation of

Friedmann's views by those of Ellul may be compared with the change in the views of David Riesman over a period:

... my collaborators and I in *The Lonely Crowd* took it for granted that it was impossible to reverse the trend towards automation; we assumed that the current efforts to make work more meaningful – which by and large succeeded only in making it more time-consuming and gregarious but not more challenging – might as well be given up, with the meaning of life to be sought henceforth in the creative use of leisure.[10]

But Riesman's subsequent consideration of research findings led him to the view that

it might be easier to make leisure more meaningful if one at the same time could make work more demanding ... It may be slightly less difficult to reorganize work routines so that they become less routine, more challenging, and hence more instructive, than to cope all at once with the burdens placed on leisure by the evaporation of the meaning of work ... I believe that we cannot take advantage of what remains of our pre-industrial heritage to make leisure more creative, individually and socially, if work is not creative, too.

The solutions put forward by Friedmann and (the early) Riesman, while based on the differentiation of work and leisure, involve only a certain degree of pessimism about 'humanizing' the former and not a desire to write it off altogether as a source of human fulfilment. A few writers, however, have suggested just that. Fairchild is quoted as saying: 'Work must be recognized not as a virtue or a blessing, but as an intrinsic evil. The only justification for work is its product ... We must come to realize that leisure time, that is, time spent in pleasurable employment, is the only kind of time that makes life worth living ...'[11] Marcuse looks forward to society being organized 'with a view to saving time and space for the development of individuality *outside* the inevitably repressive work-world.'[12] A less extreme view is held by Vincent and Mayers: 'Man faces the prospect of making work shorter and less onerous, of combining it with play, and then of making play primary and work secondary.'[13] In answering Friedmann, Ellul has also implicitly answered these writers. We may now turn to the second general answer to the problem of the confrontation of work and leisure.

Answer 2: The Integration of Work and Leisure

In earlier chapters evidence was given that work is not a central life interest for most manual and the business type of non-manual employees. In Chapter 6 attention was drawn to the apparent contradiction between a majority choice of 'home and family' as a source of central life interest and a majority choice of an 'integrated' (work and leisure) pattern of living, in connexion with a study of Japanese industrial workers. There are other indications that it would be easy to read too much into quantitative findings about sources of central life interest. Frank Friedlander concluded from his study of manual and non-manual government employees that

work and the work environment do provide greater opportunity for satisfying interactions than do nonwork factors. For example, the value to all groups of their combined work content and work context as an opportunity to obtain satisfying stimulation exceed to a significant extent that of church-related and that of educational factors ... Similarly, recreational activities were perceived as having the least value for potentially satisfying stimulation, particularly when compared with work-related activities.[14]

It is true that Friedlander's findings make no mention of home and family life as providing 'satisfying interactions', but there is probably good reason to keep the family and leisure aspects of non-work separate in the analysis of central life interest. There is a sense in which the family, as a *primary* group, is on a different level from the *secondary* group memberships involved in work and much of leisure life. Seen in this light, leisure is the true competitor of work for the individual's main source of satisfying interactions, and the evidence is that for most types of worker leisure comes off second best.

There is a further indication that the division of life into spheres which can be ranked in order of providing satisfaction is somewhat artificial. In line with the Japanese workers who favoured an ideal pattern of integrated work and leisure, a number of both manual and non-manual informants in my surveys answered the question about ambition in life in terms which spanned both work and non-work spheres, for example, 'to make my life a success' or 'to create a position where my occupation and private life are running as one'. Also, it will be remembered that a substantial minority of those interviewed on the pilot inquiry of business and service workers declined to give any one main sphere as the source of their central life interest.

Friedlander is one of the few writers who have discussed the integration of work and leisure on the basis of his own survey research. In his concluding remarks to the study quoted above, he states that 'one may well question the extent to which recreation will prove an even partial substitute for work as an opportunity for meaningful environmental interaction.' If that is true of recreation, it is probably true of the other functions of leisure. Personal development is hardly likely to be enhanced by a withdrawal from the more rewarding kind of work, since, as Wilensky points out, 'among men not accustomed to the wider universe made available by demanding work, it takes a long, expensive education to avoid an impoverished life.'[15] Hollander expresses the aim of integration: 'the long-range goal is not only to maximize leisure time but also to fuse it with a uniquely satisfying form of work. Indeed, the projected fusion of work with creativity lends a totally new complexion to the whole concept of leisure, making it more difficult to differentiate it from this new kind of work.'[16] In this fusion, work may lose its present characteristic feature of constraint and gain the creativity now associated mainly with leisure, while leisure may lose its present characteristic feature of opposition to work and gain the status – now associated mainly with the *product* of work – of a resource worthy of planning to provide the greatest possible human satisfaction.

The observers who propose an integration of work and leisure disagree with the advocates of differentiation not only in their proposed solution to the problem but also in their perception of the present state of affairs. Whereas the 'segmentalists' see work and leisure as compartments of life and society, the 'holists' see a *relationship* between present work and leisure, though not an organic one. According to Ben Seligman:

Leisure becomes a social problem when its purpose, the regeneration of the human being, is denied or debased. Regeneration can be realized only when leisure confronts work which is meaningful. Then the human spirit recoups its energies for another bout with nature. In a sense leisure is earned through such a confrontation. But under modern technology free time can be used only as an escape from the oppressiveness of the industrial system. However ... free time is itself 'industrialized'; hence there is no genuine escape. Moreover, under automation, leisure's task is to fill empty time, something that modern man does poorly anyway. The irony is that work is employed to supply leisure with objects to make the latter ostensibly enjoyable, while leisure is frequently used to advance one's status in work as on the golf course, or in the upper reaches of the corporate milieu. But there is no organic relationship here: all that is visible is a mechanistic exploitation of one realm by the other. Besides, the use of leisure as leverage in work is reserved to the upper classes in our society.[17]

It might reasonably be countered that leisure is 'frequently used to advance one's status in work' only by those who are imbued with the Protestant ethic and who do not know how to enjoy leisure for its own sake. But the point about mechanistic exploitation of one realm by the other is well taken – whether it is Aristotle's 'we labour in order to have leisure' or the industrial recreationist's 'we have leisure in order to labour better.' In individual psychological terms, too, integration of spheres may be a more stable situation and easier to maintain than a split consciousness. Kenneth Keniston writes:

The man who spends his working day at a job whose primary meaning is merely to earn enough money to enable him to enjoy the rest of his time can seldom really enjoy his leisure, his family, or his avocations. Life is of a piece, and if work is empty or routine, the rest will inevitably become contaminated as well, becoming a compulsive escape or a driven effort to compensate for the absent satisfactions that should inhere in work. Similarly, to try to avoid social and political problems by cultivating one's garden can at best be only partly successful. When the effects of government and society are so ubiquitous, one can escape them only in the backwaters, and then only for a short while. Putting work, society, and politics into one pigeonhole, and family, leisure and enjoyment into another creates a compartmentalization which is in continual danger of collapsing. Or, put more precisely, such a division of life into nonoverlapping spheres merely creates a new psychological strain, the almost impossible strain of artificially maintaining a continually split outlook.[18]

The case in favour of an integration of work and leisure turns out to be mainly a critique of what various forms of differentiation have failed to achieve. This is perhaps unavoidable at the present stage of social development. We have no set of social institutions and corresponding cultural patterns which *represent* an integration of work and leisure – we have, at most, the behaviour and attitudes of a comparatively few individuals sharing certain patterns of living which indicate what that integration could be. Even this kind of guide may be misleading, for change at the societal level is not, for example, a matter of seeking to extend the life patterns of residential social workers to embrace all kinds of workers. The wider realization of human potentialities is clearly a long-term goal, although this does not mean that we cannot take short-term steps in that direction. To reconcile work with leisure, to show how the one can enhance the other, may take some time, for we have long thought of work as the opposite of leisure. Making efforts here and there to ameliorate working conditions or to enhance the joys of leisure are valuable activities, but they may do no more than help us to hold our own against the sweeping tide of technological and marketing society. A sociological imagination that reminds us of the real range of social behaviour is necessary so that we can collectively decide which kinds of work and which kinds of leisure are appropriate to a good life, and create the opportunities for these to be realized.

Finally we come to consider the implications of what has been said in previous chapters for social policies dealing with problems of work and leisure. We shall first assess two alternative types of general policy based on contrasting social theories – segmentalist and holist. The possibilities of revaluing work and leisure as spheres of life will then be discussed. To conclude, some practical problems in planning for work and leisure will be reviewed.

Segmentalist Policies

It is possible to examine the segmentalist proposals for work and leisure in relative isolation from each other, although it may be useful to distinguish the 'neutrality' from the 'opposition' approach. As a starting point we may consider the three 'solutions to the problem of stultifying labour' outlined by Wilensky:

(1) develop patterns of creative, challenging leisure to compensate for an inevitable spread in dehumanized labour; (2) offer vastly better compensation to those condemned to alienating work situations (the trade union solution of more money for less working-time . . .); (3) redesign the workplace and the technology to invest work with more meaning, and hence enhance the quality of leisure.[1]

These three proposed solutions may be related respectively to the three patterns of work–leisure relationship: neutrality, opposition (both involving a segmentalist view of society) and extension (involving a holist view of society). Although the first solution includes the word 'compensation', and to that extent implies a recognition of some kind of relationship between work and leisure, it suggests that 'dehumanized' labour can be tolerated if it is kept separate from a creative, challenging leisure. As we have seen, there must be grave doubts about whether this can be achieved. Attempts to do so, however, appeal to those who despair of making drastic changes in the work content and environment of the mass of people, at least in the short run. The industrial recreation movement, and government and local authority sponsored sports and recreation facilities are examples of this kind of solution.

The second solution is a more straightforward acceptance that leisure is the opposite of work. Although Wilensky may not have intended to differentiate between 'dehumanized labour' in the first solution and 'alienating work situations' in the second, it may nevertheless be useful to draw some such distinction. The crucial difference appears to lie in the nature of the compensation offered. In the first case it is entirely in non-work terms: in return for acceptance of a whole package of 'dehumanized labour', a more attractive leisure package is offered. In the second case the compensation is both within and outside the work sphere: although the work situation itself is not altered, the hours of work may be shortened or the economic rewards increased. The difference between the two solutions may be expressed as society making two compensatory propositions to those whose work it recognizes to be intrinsically unpleasant or unsatisfying: (1) 'We know it's boring, but put up with it and we shall make it up to you in leisure,' or (2) 'We know it's damaging, but you need only do it for a short time and we shall pay you well for it.'

It seems likely that boring and uncreative work will be with us for longer than damaging work. Work which leaves no obvious mark on the body or the life of the employee is less likely to attract widespread criticism and demands for reform than work which is self-evidently harmful. The number of 'extreme' occupations – extreme in the sense of danger or physical strain – is diminishing. Wherever possible, machines are used to do such work, not necessarily from any humanitarian motives (though, as in the case of the abolition of slavery, these no doubt play a part) but because it is usually more economically advantageous to do so. Also, the role of the trade unions in campaigning for greater regard to be paid to health and safety questions in industry must not be overlooked. However, much less concern is expressed about work which is relatively safe and unharmful to physical health but which has a low potential for human satisfaction and feelings of creativity. The role of the time-study man, which is essentially that of a technician looking upon man as a mere tool to be 'serviced' so that he can work as rapidly and effectively as possible, is generally accepted. It is left to industrial psychologists and sociologists to insist that man has a fundamental need to participate in the work he does and to recommend that it should be organized in ways that would involve and develop and expand his personality so far as possible.

The reasons for the greater popularity of segmentalist solutions to problems of work are not hard to find. They have the obvious merit of being applicable on a small scale and do not require the amount of research and education of public opinion that would be entailed in holist solutions (to be considered presently). Segmentalist solutions aim at limited goals which are therefore more easily achieved, and their programmes tend to flow from obvious rather than imaginative comparisons. Thus the goal that workers usually set themselves (or that is set for them by their representatives) is to obtain the best possible income and working conditions which any comparable group of workers has achieved. The 'differentials' are the subject of much concern, but they are *actual* differentials between groups of workers – not the differential between existing and potential conditions given a possible re-structuring of society and its values.

The segmentalist approach to leisure is parallel with the approach to work. Since the influence on leisure of other spheres of life is discounted, attempts are made to change it as a more or less self-contained sphere. The aim to 'develop patterns of creative, challenging leisure' does not depend on the individual bringing to it values and experiences gained in other spheres of life, and so the question of *how* these new patterns of leisure are to be developed becomes important. In a society in which the provision of leisure goods and services has become a major industry, there is no great problem of access to the means of spending leisure time, assuming that one has also money to spend. For the segmentalist, a greater problem may be how to encourage people to spend their leisure time in ways which are socially acceptable, because segmentalism rarely extends to a complete unconcern with the effects on society (or, for that matter, on the individual) of 'undesirable' activities.

In Britain there is some concern about the ways in which certain groups – especially the more rebellious types of young people – spend their leisure time. The Youth Service, religious and other welfare organizations are doing something to provide leisure facilities, with or without guidance in how best to use leisure time, and there is considerable pressure on local government to do more in this field.[2] Without denying the need for such efforts, it seems that too little attention has been paid to the non-leisure determinants of leisure behaviour. Such important influences as the family and the school on leisure are outside the scope of this book, but there are plenty of indications that different occupational experiences must be taken into account in explaining patterns of leisure behaviour. For example, among young people the influence of friends and 'the gang' – strengthened by the image of appropriate (consumer) behaviour projected by advertisers and the mass media – may stimulate a more 'oppositional' reaction to stultifying work than the 'neutrality' reaction more typical of older people. As an instance of this oppositional reaction, a girl on a rampaging bank holiday trip to a seaside resort was reported as saying, 'You've got to get your kicks somehow. You've got to make up for all that boring time you're going to spend at work next week.'[3]

In America there has been developing a movement which has so far hardly started in Britain but which clearly has potentialities for crossing the Atlantic. That movement is professional recreation, and its personnel – paid and voluntary – are variously known as professional recreation workers, recreationists, leisurists, and even recreators. The main assumptions and aims of this movement have been put frankly by W. C. Sutherland: 'Since the average citizen is unable to invent new uses for his leisure, a professional elite shares a heavy responsibility for discovering criteria for ways of employing leisure and creating enthusiasms for common ends within the moral aims of the community.'[4] The key words in this statement are 'professional elite' and 'moral aims'. There is more than a touch of paternalism about the word 'elite' and it implies a situation in which only a cultivated few really know how to use leisure. The adjective 'professional' further implies that being a member of the elite may itself be a matter of education – perhaps the gaining of a university degree in professional recreation. The 'moral aims' to be pursued emphasize that only certain kinds of leisure are to be promoted and that they are intended as a means of social control. Indeed, in the sense of seeking to make leisure serve an integrative function in society, the aims of professional recreationists may be seen as holist; it is in their conception of an elitist society and of the mass of people as potential clients of their professional skills that their philosophy is essentially segmentalist.

It is perhaps significant that 'professional recreation' is a more popular description than 'professional leisure'. This may be partly because leisure is supposed to be generally informal and spontaneous, and there is an apparent paradox in professionally planning an uncommitted part of life. But recreation also implies a relationship to work, a re-creating of energies used in work. It is not surprising, therefore, that some advocates of professional recreation have an ambivalent attitude to work. Thus James Charlesworth believes that the recreationist 'must have the courage to pronounce that work-for-work's sake is philosophically bad and can only result in mortification of the spirit and the flesh.'[5] Presumably it is thought that work not for its own sake but as a means to something else, such as earning a living, will not result in such 'mortification'.

Holist Policies

In contrast to the kind of policies considered above, holist policies are concerned with the patterning of society as a whole. Although they may embody specific proposals for dealing with work or leisure problems, they do so within a framework of thought that recognizes the interdependence of spheres. Indeed, their advocates may go further in suggesting that part of the problem may lie in the very split between spheres and, unlike the advocates of segmentalism, may point to the costs rather than the gains to the individual of such a split. Inevitably their policies are longer-term than segmentalist ones, since they involve wider repercussions on established standards of behaviour and values. In their effect on the social structure they are revolutionary rather than reformist, and hence are open to the pros and cons that are generally put forward in connexion with these alternative ways of changing society.

Most holist policies for dealing with work and leisure have a basis in work, since those who put them forward tend to share the view that leisure is itself a creation of our industrial system. With this proviso, concepts that apply to both work and leisure spheres have a special value to holist policies. One such concept is the 'productive orientation' put forward by Erich Fromm.[6] This refers to the active and creative relatedness of man to his fellow man, to himself and to nature, and is expressed in the realms of thought, feeling and action. The productive orientation is set against both the exploitative and the hoarding orientation (the exploitation of man by man and the pleasure in possession and property, dominant in the nineteenth century) and the receptive and marketing orientation (the passive 'drinking in' of commodities and the experience of oneself as a thing to be employed successfully on the market, dominant today). The receptive and marketing orientation sums up a situation of alienation from both work and leisure. In contrast, the productive orientation sums up a situation in which people *participate* in what they do, whether it is called work or leisure. Such an orientation is implicit in Michael Harrington's belief that 'there could be a new kind of leisure and a new kind of work, or more precisely a range of activities that would partake of the nature of both leisure and work.'[7]

A number of writers have suggested that one of the chief barriers to a closer integration of work and leisure is the preoccupation of our society with production at the expense of other values, and the individual preference for more income at the expense of more leisure time. The economist Alan Day has pointed out that much the greater part of the benefit of rising productivity has been taken out in the form of more money to buy more goods, and very little in the form of increased leisure through shorter working hours.[8] Bearing in mind the growth of hire purchase and the power of the mass media to stimulate wants which need higher incomes to satisfy them, there is no reason to look for an early reversal of this trend. Also, many workers in America who lack definite ideas about what to do with increased leisure time seem to prefer the same number of working days rather than more days in which they are expected by their wives to do small tasks around the home. Day notes that some of the benefits of automation and mechanization are now enjoyed in the form not of higher productivity but of more pleasant working conditions. Easing off on the job so as to have more time for a smoke or a gossip may constitute a 'restrictive practice' from a purely economic point of view, but may, from the worker's point of view, be a reduction in the split between work (which is something unpleasant and has to be tolerated) and leisure (which is isolated and pleasurable).

Day suggests that rising productivity might allow us to 'deliberately choose methods of production which may not necessarily be the most "efficient" but still contribute most to human happiness'. There is certainly plenty of scope for increasing this contribution to happiness so far as the average worker today is concerned. It is true that considerable progress has been made over the last fifty years in improving the physical environment of the worker. When factories are built nowadays attention is paid to proper lighting, temperature, noise control, ventilation, and even decorative colour schemes. Standards in office building and equipment have also improved. These developments have been partly the result of management's awareness that a good work environment promotes efficiency, and partly the result of the pressure of organized labour. But even if the standards reached by the best firms today are eventually achieved by the others, all this does not change the *content* of the work and what it *means* to the people who have to do it. If the achievements of the past fifty years were concentrated on the physical environment of work, attention over the next fifty years must turn increasingly to the quality of working life itself – the social relationships of work and the opportunities it gives for personal fulfilment.

It is too often thought to be a matter of little or no importance that most jobs today – or, more precisely, the way they are organized and the conditions under which they are done – afford no satisfaction and are even sources of misery and frustration. Mr John Newton, in his presidential address to the 1969 Trades

Union Congress, drew attention to some of the human costs of the present industrial system:

> Where work gives little or no satisfaction to the worker, where there is no freedom to exercise talent or skill, where men and women do not determine how they do their work, where they have become merely components in the production system, they have, during their working lives, lost their identity as individuals. . . .
>
> Nobody who has not experienced the effects of years of confinement within the walls of mass production, without apparent means of escape, can understand the debilitating effects on the mind, the vocabulary, on the spiritual capacity of human endurance. Nobody, without this experience, can really understand why men down tools, when on the surface there seems to be only a pretext, to escape momentarily from the monotony of an unnatural existence.

Perhaps those responsible for planning and running industry will be forced to turn their attention to improving the experience of work only when other methods of preventing workers from downing tools through boredom and frustration have failed. It will be a pity if progress in this direction has to come from a concern with production rather than with making working lives more worthwhile, but the *achievement* of change is more important than the motives that prompt it.

It is sometimes said that we have put the Victorian 'work morality' behind us because we allow that work need no longer be the sole preoccupation of life. But in another sense this morality lives on. We are continually brainwashed with ideas about increasing productivity, the balance of payments, restoring confidence in the pound, and so on. But none of these things really touches the quality of life of the average person. Are we to go on for ever working for the greater glory of the gross national product? Are we to become increasingly the paying customers of the leisure industries? To pose these questions is not to assert that collectively we can consume more than we produce, nor is it to deny the continuing need to harness technical knowledge and scientific advance to the benefit of man. But it *is* to challenge the assumption that the present economic and social organization of our affairs, with its own peculiar priorities, is the most appropriate one to meet our needs.

Imaginative critics of the present order point to the integration of work and leisure now experienced by some employees as something that could be extended to the lives of others. Thus Kenneth Denbigh writes: 'Surely it should be one of the important functions of industry in society that the employment it gives should be such that a man can put into his work a great deal of himself. Professional people take it for granted that their own work is of this kind.'[9] A holist consideration that the raising of levels of consumption will eventually call into question the quality of the work environment leads Denbigh to assert that 'there will surely come a time when the world will want some new kind of productive system – one which will yield, as well as the output of goods, more rewarding conditions in their making.'[10] It is unlikely that 'the world' will suddenly decide it wants such a system. Much more probably, a growing number of people, having achieved better material standards of living, will turn their attention to improving their lives in other ways, including demanding for themselves and others working lives worthy of whole persons and not merely of hired hands.

What do holist policies imply for the actual content and conditions of work and leisure? Apart from deliberately introducing leisure-like experiences into the working day (thereby somewhat blurring the distinction between work and leisure) certain policies with regard to the organization of work are also relevant. Greater autonomy in their own jobs and greater participation in the way the enterprise as a whole is run are two of the main ways in which holist policies would benefit employees. Giving people more autonomy in their work should help to reconcile work with leisure, since this is a feature of jobs that has been shown to be associated with the 'extension' pattern. Democratic participation in the running of industrial and commercial enterprises is important because it is likely to be accompanied by democratic participation in running the affairs of the community.

It is possible to approach the twin problems of work and leisure from the angle of leisure as well as that of work. Instead of starting with concepts such as the 'productive orientation' or 'shared responsibilities', which stem mainly from work, we can inquire what is the optimum role of leisure in life and society and then seek to integrate this with other spheres, including work. Leisure as the opposite of work, that is, leisure as detachment, passivity, and general absence of effort is not reconcilable with work, but leisure as interest, pleasurable activity, and a general sense of creative self-expression can be seen as continuous with some aspects of work. Our aim can thus include the growth of leisure time in which to do the work we wish. The integration of work and leisure means more than just introducing a few bits of leisure-like activity into certain restricted parts of the working day – it means a whole new pattern of daily activities. In the words of Ahtik Vitomir, 'this trend towards the integration of different fields of activity will be reflected in the desire to reduce the duality between work and leisure, between private and public activity, between intellectual and artistic, mental and physical concerns, etc.'[11]

Revaluing Work and Leisure

A major difference between segmentalist and holist policies is that the former deal with the implications of changes in only one segment at a time, assuming everything else to be constant, whereas the latter deal with the impact of change in any part of system on the system as a whole. Although the field of policy is one in which it would be foolish to deny the role of value judgments about what is desirable there is a sense in which the very structure of complex social interrelationships determines the extent of repercussions of change initiated at any one point. Segmentalism 'works' to the extent that the spheres of society (or of the individual's life) *are* actually segmented, but it fails to the extent that change in a part affects the whole. These considerations have special relevance to the problem of values attached to work and leisure.

Any revaluation of work and leisure must first of all involve a redefinition of the terms, or at least a change of emphasis in their meaning. In Chapter 2 it was shown that employment is only one kind of work and that, since leisure means choice, time spent from choice in work activity can be leisure just as much as can the more usual leisure activities. By policies which introduce leisure-like elements into employment situations, and by refusing to define leisure as a separate period in which no work is done, the present largely opposite conceptions of work and leisure may give way to a situation in which we can say 'Work must be pleasure, too'. However, it is not necessary – nor perhaps even desirable – to aim at complete fusion of work and leisure so that they become indistinguishable. As long as there are discrepancies between individual needs or aims and the needs (i.e. best interests) of society as a whole, there will continue to be some measure of constraint on at least some of the time of most of the people. The basic distinction between instrumental (means) activities and expressive (end) activities, and differences in degrees of constraint or choice, will mean that some such terms as work and leisure will continue to have relevance, though probably not such sharply differentiated meanings as they have for most people today. Also, it must not be forgotten that leisure as freedom from constraint can be a counter both to work and to non-work obligations. 'Leisure can become a breaking-away in two senses. It is a stoppage of activities required by the job, or family or social responsibilities, and at the same time a sharp questioning of the routine stereotypes and ready-made notions resulting from the repetitiveness and specialization of day-to-day responsibilities.'[12]

Two developments in modern industry have implications for a revaluation of work and leisure. The first concerns the change in the occupational structure which has been taking place in recent decades. Automatic processes are taking the place of operators of repetitive machines, clerical drudges and workers on assembly lines, and more people are engaged in professional and service-type occupations. These changes should, in the long run, reduce the proportion of employees who feel alienated from their work. M. A. Fried has shown that the concept of what is work undergoes change as occupations develop in terms of such factors as advanced training, skills and abilities required.[13] At the lowest level, work is just a *job* involving subordination to other people. It may then become a *task* allowing some pleasure and pride in performance. As an *occupation* work includes not only task-pleasure but also provides opportunities for developing responsibility for, and identity with, an overall integrated work goal. Finally, a *career* may enable people to identify their own personal achievement with their work and to make social participation and individual fulfilment almost indistinguishable. The occupational structure is tending to provide more careers and opportunities for people to have that kind of relationship to their work.

A second development making for a revaluation of work and leisure is the reduction in working hours which the mass of people may expect. Estimates of the probable rate of reduction vary, but few question the direction of the trend.[14] It is mainly these two developments that have led George Soule to claim that, 'paradoxically, our civilization is clearing the way for meaningful and voluntary work by maximising leisure.'[15] As automation and service occupations make it more and more difficult to measure the output of a single individual, the purely economic function of work to the employee is called into question. We have already reached the stage when it is becoming increasingly unrealistic to expect everyone to 'pay' for everything he consumes from the income gained by a measured contribution to society. It used to be only the owners of capital who were subsidized by the efforts of working people; today, other non-producers or virtual non-producers in the ranks of the 'employed' are getting their more modest share. Our outmoded economic system pays financial geniuses, pop stars, and so on, their absurdly inflated market price, but it also employs machine-minders for machines that do not need minding and clerks for paperwork that could be drastically reduced in a saner system. H. A. Rhee asks 'Will not a largely automated, labour-saving, management-saving, organization-saving, post-industrial society of the future, find it necessary, first to devise new ways of distributing society's wealth and, secondly, to enable people to enjoy the satisfactions derived from work?'[16] Unless we persist in being irrational about organizing the social and economic aspects of our society, the long-term answer must be in the affirmative, and our short-term problem is to work out how to move in that direction.

Planning for Work and Leisure

If the realization of human potentialities in work and leisure is to be pursued as a social aim, there arises the question of how the relevant policies may be shaped and administered and what part sociologists can play in this. It is true, as M. Bressler points out, that 'sociologists *qua* sociologists have no special gifts as definers of public welfare.'[17] However, this does not mean that sociological theory and research has nothing to contribute to policy making. Within industry sociologists can convey to management, unions and employees the results and conclusions of investigations into the effects on workers' attitudes of variables in the work situation such as authority structure, type of technology and style of supervision. Those in a position to initiate or press for changes in these respects may do so in the reasonable expectation that corresponding changes in attitudes will result. In the realm of leisure, sociologists can obtain and convey to both the consumers and the providers of leisure goods and services information concerning the needs of people in various situations and the factors which have combined to produce those needs. Even more importantly, sociologists can join with psychologists, philosophers, historians, administrators and others in making the general public aware of the possibilities of *social* development that technological development is opening up. Large numbers of students and organized workers are showing increasing militancy in seeking some degree of control over the conditions of their educational and working lives. These campaigns may be seen as the spearhead of a wider movement towards a type of society which not only allows but encourages democratic participation by all its members.

Any programme for the realization of human potentialities must be based on the satisfaction of need, but the concept of need may be interpreted in various ways. Needs vary from the purely physiological to the most socially determined. Some needs are basic to life itself and their satisfaction occupies an irreducible minimum of any individual's time budget. At the other end of the scale are needs which are least basic to life itself but are said to express most fully the character of civilized man. Just as individual man has to satisfy his basic needs before he can concern himself with 'higher things', so society has first to meet the basic needs of all its members before it can provide leisure for even a section of them. But to see a straight-line progression from all labour (distinguished from both work and leisure, in Arendt's sense) to all leisure is to distort the picture.

The weight of historical, anthropological and contemporary evidence is that, whatever their expressed desires, men in all societies *need* to have work as well as leisure. Further, in cases where their work embodies many of the values normally associated with leisure, a separate period of time labelled leisure appears to be necessary neither to their own happiness nor to their creative function in society.

The central problem, then, is not one of maximizing some values (i.e. those associated with leisure) and minimizing others (associated with work) but of achieving an integration of both sets of values. Integration of another kind is also necessary: that between the needs of individuals and of society. It is this latter kind of integration that poses the most problems to those concerned with planning for work and leisure, since it is only in a metaphorical sense that society has 'needs' apart from those of its individual members. Neither the needs for work nor those for leisure are easy to determine on a societal scale, and the latter are particularly difficult. It is fairly easy to see what kinds of work fulfil expressive needs, because the kinds of work that do not are undertaken only instrumentally. But with leisure there is no such criterion to employ – it is *all* supposed to be expressive.

Alfred Willener writes that 'true leisure ought to be free, "natural", it cannot be engineered.'[18] This is the *laissez-faire* doctrine of leisure as free time, apparently not determined by anyone other than the leisure user himself but in fact quite markedly mediated by various social influences, for example, those of the mass media and of advertisers. It is true that the person who is sufficiently self-contained may resist these influences and, provided he has resources developed in other spheres of life, create for himself an autonomous leisure. But for the mass of people who play no greater part in determining the conditions of their leisure than in determining the conditions of their work, the choice is not between having the use of leisure engineered or not engineered; it is between having it engineered by various agencies, with various degrees of persuasive power and with various motives of those doing the persuading.[19] At present we appear to be content to let the provision of leisure facilities, and even the very ideas about how leisure should be spent, be guided by a kind of 'invisible hand', which produces results in the leisure field comparable to those produced by the same *laissez-faire* doctrine in the industrial field. Social improvements do not just come about. Priorities have to be determined and efforts for their achievement kept up.

There is surely a parallel to be drawn between planning in the industrial sphere and planning in the leisure sphere. The recognition that unregulated *laissez-faire* is not the best way to reconcile supply and demand, even within a market economy, led to the intervention of the state and its increasingly important role as supreme planner. However, in Western countries the role of the state is limited, and decisions at a lower level than those of national policy are left in the hands of individuals or groups, though these decisions are to a large extent shaped by the interplay of economic factors and not by individual will. The parallel with leisure lies in the possibility of state or other collective intervention in decisions which affect the facilities provided for leisure, but in such a way that individual autonomy and development would be promoted rather than diminished. Most of us would agree that we should not try to direct people's energies into channels specified in advance. We should aim instead to nourish the individual's potentialities so that each, according to his capacity, could find his own solution. Unfortunately, as Raymond Aron points out, 'all societies, including the wealthiest continue to train *the men they need* but ... none, despite its proclaimed objectives, *needs* to have all men realize fully their individual potentialities. No society *needs* to have many men become personalities fully capable of freedom in relation to their environment.'[20] The message is plain enough: if we do not press for opportunities to realize our individual potentialities, no one else is going to do it for us. This especially goes for working life – neither the government, nor the employers, nor even the trade unions, are there to develop us as persons. Various pressure groups may be made, at least partially, to serve this end but the impetus must come from ourselves.

Traditional planning considered that leisure was the luxury of the few and that for the masses work came first and whatever was left over was free time to be passed as 'wholesomely' – and as cheaply to the community – as possible. Such a concept of planning survives today and concentrates on the requirements of the work environment, giving high priority to efficient physical relationships among factories, offices, schools, shops, houses and transport routes. The residual 'open space' that remains is regarded as adequate to meet leisure requirements. Very little attention has been paid by planners to a positive approach to leisure by understanding and forecasting leisure-time behaviour, and by developing resources in line with estimated demand. Moreover, there has been almost no concern with how this demand is shaped – planning has taken notice of vested interests and pressure groups but not of what might be called the needs for individual, personal development.

The key institution in this neglected process of collective planning for individual development is that of education. The idea has recently been gaining ground that the schools should teach leisure subjects to young people who are probably going into kinds of work that they will not make their central life interest. William Faunce predicts, as one of the social consequences of automation, that 'in the long run the primary responsibility of the schools may well become that of instilling certain kinds of values and interests which permit the creative use of leisure and, in general, the teaching not of vocational but of leisure skills.'[21] This is an example of the segmentalist approach, though if the subjects are taught in such a way that they generate needs and values which react on what is expected from and achieved in work it can be valuable. More importantly, from a holist point of view there is the possibility of teaching subjects in such a way that they are means neither to work nor to leisure but express *ends* in both spheres.

Finally, we may consider a further aspect of the role of the sociologist in planning for work and leisure. It has already been noted that, in providing certain facts about human needs and satisfactions, sociologists and others may indirectly influence those having some responsibility for the way people work and spend their leisure time. At this level the role of values may be kept fairly neutral. It need not be a matter of saying. 'We want you to make these changes because we think they would be good for people.' The advice may be limited to the relatively value-free type of '*If* you do this, *then* that is likely to result.' The qualification 'relatively' is necessary because the selection of a course of action the results of which are to be predicted itself represents a priority choice from among a number of possible courses of action.

Apart from this type of dispassionate advice, there are the methods of 'active sociology' which some French sociologists advocate. Active sociology

holds that the social subject, though determined by a situation, has at the same time the power to determine the situation by a conscious and voluntary policy . . . it is not a question of conducting a historical study of the past but of selecting, from among all the processes of evolution, those which correspond to explicit criteria of development and of making a prognosis of their probable projection in the short or long term, according to one or more possible courses of action . . .[22]

'Criteria of development' clearly imply a value-choice, but once selected they can lead on to a more strictly sociological process of analysing the nature of the interaction of various social forces. Thus leisure may be seen as 'a factor for cultural progress or cultural decline, for social integration or alienation, it may stimulate the involvement of the individual or lead him into irresponsibility towards himself and his kind.' We may first choose which of these alternatives we think preferable, analyse its sources and manifestations, and then take appropriate action to achieve the desired ends. A similar procedure may be followed with regard to the sphere of work.

It may be helpful to review the main points made in these last two chapters from the standpoint of active sociology. Most of this book has been devoted to showing that there are types of relationship between work and leisure to be seen on the levels both of individual life spheres and social organization. To attribute the main reason for these differences either to types of person or to types of social situation has important implications for policy. In the one case attempts will be made to fit persons seeking (or not seeking) fulfilment in work to jobs capable (or incapable) of providing that fulfilment; in the other case attempts will be made, through more far-reaching changes, to give everyone the chance of experiencing the same encouragement to development through work. In the field of leisure the one policy will be to provide leisure facilities for the 'type of people' who need them; the other to stimulate an awareness of the possibilities of leisure-like behaviour in a variety of situations.

The choice between two main schools of thought about the relation of life spheres in urban-industrial society is also important. Segmentalists will want to tackle the problems of work and leisure in relative isolation from each other, on the assumption that differentiation of spheres makes this possible; holists will want to pursue a more difficult and longer-term policy of integration, on the assumption that the interdependence of spheres makes this necessary. At the level of general theories of society there are again implications for policy. Those accepting a segmentalist theory of the nature of society and social change will want to make 'practical' reforms to the existing work and leisure spheres starting with the experiences and immediate environments of individuals; those accepting a holist theory of society will insist that more far-reaching policies aimed at changes in the social and economic structure as a whole are necessary.

Any specific changes in the content, organization and environment of work and leisure will depend for their success on accompanying changes in the relevant social values or philosophy. The key institution in any process of revaluation is that of education, both in the schools and in adult life. In the schools boys and girls may be taught in such ways that subjects are not regarded as 'vocational' and 'non-vocational' (narrowly vocational subjects are, in any case, training rather than education) and then encouraged to expect more from any job they choose than just the pay packet.

It may be that some people will still choose to invest relatively little of themselves in their work and may see it only as a means to enjoying leisure, but at least the options will have been open. Collective action to achieve, beyond better pay and conditions, more rewarding work for all would reinforce the process of critical evaluation started in the schools. In the field of leisure provision, the consumer would be encouraged to expect something more than routine diversion, though this should not imply an indiscriminate bias against popular entertainment and in favour of 'high culture'. The important thing is to make available opportunities for rewarding work and for the various kinds of leisure that complement rewarding work. The extent to which advantage is taken of such opportunities must, of course, remain the choice of the individual.

Notes

2 PROBLEMS OF DEFINITION

1. H. Arendt, *The Human Condition*, Chicago University Press, 1958, p. 127.

2. J. Keenan, 'On the Dole', in R. Fraser (ed.), Work: *Twenty Personal Accounts*, Harmondsworth, Middx.: Penguin Books in association with New Left Review, 1968, p. 276.

3. G. Hunter, *Work and Leisure*, London: Central Committee of Study Groups, 1961, p. 16.

4. G. Soule, 'The Economics of Leisure', *Annals of the American Academy of Political and Social Science*, Sept. 1957.

5. H. P. Fairchild (ed.), *Dictionary of Sociology*, New York: Philosophical Library, 1944.

6. E. Gross, 'A Functional Approach to Leisure Analysis', *Social Problems*, Summer 1961.

7. G. A. Lundberg *et al.*, *Leisure – A Suburban Study*, New York: Columbia University Press, 1934, p. 2.

8. A. Giddens, 'Notes on the Concept of Play and Leisure', *Sociological Review*, March 1964.

9. R. C. White, 'Social Class Differences in the Use of Leisure', *American Journal of Sociology*, Sept. 1955.

10. C. K. Brightbill, *The Challenge of Leisure*, New York: Prentice-Hall, 1963, p. 4.

11. N. P. Gist and S. F. Fava, *Urban Society*, New York: Crowell, 1964, p. 411.

12. J. Dumazedier, 'Current Problems of the Sociology of Leisure', *International Social Science Journal*, No. 4, 1960.

13. M. Kaplan, *Leisure in America*, New York: Wiley, 1960, p. 22.

14. K. Vontobel, *Das Arbeitsethos des deutschen Protestantismus*, Bern: Francke, 1945, p. 83 (quoted in N. Anderson, *Work and Leisure*, London: Routledge, 1961, p. 33).

15. J. Pieper, *Leisure the Basis of Culture*, London: Faber, 1952.

16. S. DeGrazia, *Of Time, Work and Leisure*, New York: Twentieth Century Fund, 1962, pp. 7–8.

17. H. Marcuse, *One-Dimensional Man*, London: Routledge, 1964, p. 49.

18. In addition to the schemes by Brightbill, *op. cit.*, and DeGrazia, *op. cit.*, see N. Anderson and K. Ishwaran, *Urban Sociology*, London: Asia Publishing House, 1965, p. 93; G. Friedmann, 'Leisure and Technological Civilization', *Internationl Social Science Journal*, No. 4, 1960, p. 514; A. Szalai *et al.*, 'The Multinational Comparative Time Budget Research Project', report to Sixth World Congress of Sociology, Evian, 1966, p. 35; and British Travel Association – University of Keele, *Pilot National Recreation Survey*, Report No. 1, July 1967, pp. 25–26.

19. H. Gavron, London: Routledge, 1966.

20. A. Szalai, 'Differential Evaluation of Time Budgets for Comparative Purposes', in R. L. Merritt and S. Rokkan (eds.), *Comparing Nations*, New Haven: Yale University Press, 1966, p. 245.

3 WORK AND LEISURE IN HISTORY AND OTHER SOCIETIES

1. Marshall McLuhan, *Understanding Media*, London: Routledge, 1964, p. 149.

2. This summary of various historical meanings of work draws heavily upon A. Tilgher's *Work: What It Has Meant to Men through the Ages*, London: Harrap, 1931. Parallel accounts of the meaning of work in pre-capitalist society may be found in W. Sombart, *The Quintessence of Capitalism*, London: Unwin, 1915, pp. 18–19, and in the period of the Reformation up to the nineteenth century in H. E. Barnes, *Social Institutions*, New York: Prentice-Hall, 1946, pp. 804–5, and A. Heckscher, *The Public Happiness*. London: Hutchinson, 1963, pp. 160–163. See also the summary of Tilgher in C. Wright Mills, *White Collar*, New York: Oxford University Press, 1956, pp. 215–218.

3. N. Elias and E. Dunning, 'The Quest for Excitement in Unexciting Societies', paper presented to British Sociological Association Conference, London, 1967.

4. T. Veblen, *The Theory of the Leisure Class*, London: Allen and Unwin, 1925, p. 36f.

5. B. R. Salz, 'The Human Element in Industrialization', *Economic Development and Cultural Change*, Oct. 1955.

6. H. A. Rhee, *Office Automation in Social Perspective*, Oxford: Blackwell, 1968, p. 207.

7. A. Heckscher, *op. cit.*, p. 161.

8. R. H. Wax, 'Free Time in Other Cultures', in W. Donahue *et al.*

(eds.), *Free Time: Challenge to Later Maturity*, Ann Arbor: University of Michigan Press, 1958, p. 4.

9. H. Ashton, *The Basuto*, London: Oxford University Press, 1967, p. 131.

10. R. H. Wax, *op. cit.*, pp. 9–10.

11. *Ibid.*, pp. 11–12

12. E. Z. Vogt, *Modern Homesteaders*, Cambridge, Mass.: Harvard University Press, 1955, p. 114.

4 THE EXPERIENCE AND MEANING OF WORK TODAY

1. The main report on findings from my surveys is in Chapter 7.

2. Ed. R. Fraser, Harmondsworth, Middx.: Penguin Books in association with *New Left Review*, 1968–9.

3. See also Chapter 7.

4. For a summary of these (up to 1964) see S. R. Parker, 'Work Satisfaction: A Review of the Literature', *Government Social Survey Methodological Paper no. 115*, London, 1964.

5. R. S. Weiss and R. L. Kahn, 'Definitions of Work and Occupations', *Social Problems*, Fall 1960.

6. E. A. Friedmann and R. J. Havighurst, *The Meaning of Work and Retirement*, Chicago: University Press, 1954.

7. N. Morse and R. Weiss, 'The Function and Meaning of Work and the Job', *American Sociological Review*. April, 1955.

8. P. L. Berger, *The Human Shape of Work*, New York: Macmillan, pp. 218–219.

9. S. T. Boggs, 'The Values of Laboratory Workers', *Human Organization*, Fall 1963.

10. P. L. Berger, *op. cit.*, p. 217.

11. R. Blauner, *Alienation and Freedom*, Chicago: University Press, 1964.

5 KINDS OF LEISURE AND THEIR MEANING TODAY

1. These social purposes may be compared with the 'functional problems of social systems' put forward by Talcott Parsons and his associates – pattern maintenance and tension management, adaptation, goal attainment and integration. See E. Gross, 'A Functional Approach to Leisure Analysis', *Social Problems*, Summer, 1961.

2. Report of Trades Union Congress, 1965, p. 413.

3. P. Hollander, 'The Uses of Leisure', *Survey*, July 1966.

4. J. Dumazedier, *Toward a Society of Leisure*, London: Collier-Macmillan, 1967, pp. 14–17.

5. H. Wilensky, 'Work, Careers and Social Integration', *International Social Science Journal*, No. 4, 1960.

6. W. A. Faunce, 'Automation and Leisure', in H. B. Jacobson and J. S. Roucek (eds.), *Automation and Society*, New York: Philosophical Library, 1959.

7. A. Giddens, 'Notes on the Concept of Play and Leisure', *Sociological Review*, Mar. 1964.

8. J. Dumazedier and N. Latouche, 'Work and Leisure in French Sociology', *Industrial Relations*, Feb. 1962.

9. G. A. Lundberg *et al.*, *Leisure – A Suburban Study*, New York: Columbia University Press, 1934, pp. 100–101.

10. H. L. Wilensky, 'The Uneven Distribution of Leisure', *Social Problems*, Summer, 1961.

11. H. Strzeminska, 'Socio-Professional Structure and Time-Budgets', report to Sixth World Congress of Sociology, Evian, 1966, pp. 7–8, 13–14.

12. British Travel Association – University of Keele, *Pilot National Recreation Survey – Report No. 1*, July 1967.

13. K. K. Sillitoe, *Planning for Leisure*, London: H.M.S.O., 1969, p. 50.

14. J. E. Gerstl, 'Leisure Taste and Occupational Milieu', *Social Problems*, Summer 1961.

15. S. Graham, 'Social Correlates of Adult Leisure-Time Behaviour', in M. B. Sussman (ed.), *Community Structure and Analysis*, New York: Crowell, 1959, p. 347.

16. R. C. White, 'Social Class Differences in the Use of Leisure', *American Journal of Sociology*, Sept. 1955.

17. L. Reissman, 'Class, Leisure and Social Participation', *American Sociological Review*, Feb. 1954.

18. A. C. Clarke, 'The Use of Leisure and its Relation to Levels of Occupational Prestige', *American Sociological Review*, June 1956.

19. E. H. Blakelock, 'A Durkheimian Approach to Some Temporal Problems of Leisure', *Social Problems*, Summer 1961.

20. R. Aron, 'On Leisure in Industrial Societies', in J. Brooks *et al.*, *The One and the Many: the Individual in the Modern World*, New York: Harper and Row, 1962, pp. 157, 171.

21. R. J. Havighurst, 'The Leisure Activities of the Middle Aged', *American Journal of Sociology*, Sept. 1957.

22. M. N. Donald and R. J. Havighurst, 'The Meanings of Leisure', *Social Forces*, May 1959.

23. R. J. Havighurst, 'The Nature and Values of Meaningful Free-Time Activity', in R. W. Kleemeier (ed.), *Aging and Leisure*, New York: Oxford University Press, 1961.

24. R. J. Havighurst and K. Feigenbaum, 'Leisure and Life-Style', *American Journal of Sociology*, Jan. 1959.

6 WORK AND LEISURE TODAY

1. J. Tunstall, *The Fishermen*, London: MacGibbon and Kee, 1962, p. 137.

2. G. Friedmann, 'Leisure and Technological Civilization', *International Social Science Journal*, No. 4, 1960.

3. J. E. Gerstl and S. P. Hutton, *Engineers: the Anatomy of a Profession*, London: Tavistock, 1966, pp. 138–139.

4. A. Heckscher and S. DeGrazia, 'Executive Leisure', *Harvard Business Review*, July 1959.

5. D. Riesman, 'Some Observations on Changes in Leisure Attitudes', *Antioch Review*, No. 4, 1952.

6. E. F. Vogel, *Japan's New Middle Class*, Berkeley: University of California Press, 1963, p. 21.

7. K. P. Etzkorn, 'Leisure and Camping: The Social Meaning of a Form of Public Recreation', *Sociology and Social Research*, Oct. 1964.

8. F. H. Blum, *Toward a Democratic Work Process*, New York: Harper, 1953, pp. 109–110.

9. Ministry of Housing and Local Government Urban Planning Directorate, 'Provision of Playing Pitches in New Towns', 1967 (limited circulation).

10. T. Yukawa, 'Employee Recreation Program and Facilities', *Proceedings of the First World Recreation Congress*, Japan: Osaka, Oct. 1964, pp. 186–188.

11. J. M. Anderson, *Industrial Recreation*, New York: McGraw-Hill, 1955, p. 15.

12. T. Woody, 'Leisure in the Light of History', *Annals of the American Academy of Political and Social Science*, Sept. 1957.

13. P. Cullen, 'Whither Industrial Recreation Now?', Part II, *Sport and Recreation*, Jan. 1967.

14. R. Dubin, 'Industrial Workers' Worlds', *Social Problems*, Jan. 1956.

15. L. Orzack, 'Work as a "Central Life Interest" of Professionals', *Social Problems*, Fall 1959.

16. A. Kornhauser, *Mental Health of the Industrial Worker*, New York: Wiley, 1965, p. 194.

17. P. Lafitte, *Social Structure and Personality in the Factory*, London: Routledge, 1958, p. 180.

18. J. Dumazedier, *Toward a Society of Leisure*, London: Collier-Macmillan, 1967, p. 97.

19. K. Odaka, 'Work and Leisure: As Viewed by Japanese Industrial Workers', paper presented to Sixth World Congress of Sociology, Evian, 1966.

20. H. Wilensky, 'Mass Society and Mass Culture: Interdependence or Independence?', *American Sociological Review*, Apr. 1964.

21. H. Marcuse, *One-Dimensional Man*, London: Routledge, 1964, p. 74.

22. G. P. Stone, 'American Sports: Play and Dis-play', in E. Larrabee and R. Meyersohn (eds.), *Mass Leisure*, Glencoe: Free Press, 1958, p. 285.

23. D. Riesman and W. Blomberg, 'Work and Leisure: Fusion or Polarity?', in C. M. Arensberg *et al.* (eds.), *Research in Industrial Human Relations*, New York: Harper, 1957, p. 93.

24. D. Riesman, *The Lonely Crowd*, New York: Doubleday, 1953, p. 185.

25. I. Howe, 'Notes on Mass Culture', *Politics*, Spring, 1948.

26. D. Bell, 'Work in the Life of an American', in W. Haber *et al.*, (eds.), *Manpower in the United States*, New York: Harper, 1954, p. 20.

7 SOME STUDIES OF PARTICULAR GROUPS

1 S. R. Parker, *Work and Leisure; A Study of their Interrelation*, University of London Ph.D. thesis 1968.

2. P. M. Blau and W. R. Scott, *Formal Organizations*, London: Routledge, 1963, p. 43. Twenty people in each of the following occupations were interviewed. *Business:* accountants (qualified and unqualified, in practices and working in commercial organizations), advertising employees, bank employees, insurance employees, retail salespeople. *Service*: almoners, child care officers, mental welfare officers, teachers (in various types of schools and universities), youth employment officers.

3. R. L. and I. H. Simpson, 'Values, Personal Influence and Occupational Choice', *Social Forces*, Dec. 1960.

4. T. Burns and G. M. Stalker, *The Management of Innovation*, London: Tavistock, 1961, pp. 119–122.

5. R. Dubin, 'Industrial Workers' Worlds', *Social Problems*, Jan. 1956.

6. The main defects of this survey concerned the inadequate method of sampling and the low response rate, which suggested that those who replied may not have been typical of all manual workers.

7. Quoted from unpublished results by permission of Dr D. F. Swift.

8. See Chapter 2 under 'Definitions of Leisure'.

9. Harmondsworth, Middx.: Penguin Books in association with *New Left Review*, 1968, p. 8.

10. L. Moss and S. R. Parker, *The Local Government Councillor*, London: H.M.S.O., 1967.

11. Two-thirds of councillors aged 65 and over are retired.

12. 53% and 16% of manual-worker councillors were asked to stand by political parties and trade unions respectively. The corresponding figures for small employees, managers and farmers were 22% and 1%.

8 TOWARDS A THEORY OF WORK–LEISURE RELATIONSHIPS

1. A. McClung Lee, *Multivalent Man,* New York: Braziller, 1966.

2. C. M. Arensberg, 'Work and the Changing American Scene', in *Research in Industrial Human Relations*, New York: Harper, 1957.

3. P. L. Berger, *The Human Shape of Work*, New York: Macmillan, 1964, p. 219.

4. A. Etzioni, *A Comparative Analysis of Complex Organizations*, Glencoe: Free Press, 1961, pp. 9–11.

5. Staffan Linder has recently noted that economic development has resulted in an increasing *scarcity* of time and that, since there is an idea that the compulsion to work confers a greater value on the individual than the freedom to consume, the problem of scarcity of time is a psychological one. (*The Harried Leisure Class,* New York: Columbia University Press, 1970, pp. 10–12.)

6. See Chapter 5 under 'Social and Individual Functions of Leisure'.

7. H. Wilensky, 'Work Careers and Social Integration', *International Social Science Journal*, No. 4, 1960.

9 THE POTENTIALITIES OF WORK AND LEISURE

1. J. M. Fraser, *Industrial Psychology*, Oxford: Pergamon Press, 1962, pp. 176–177.
2. H. W. Durant, *The Problem of Leisure*, London: Routledge, 1938, p. 250.
3. T. Burns, 'A meaning in Everyday Life', *New Society*, 25 May 1967.
4. P. Weiss, 'A Philosophical Definition of Leisure', in *Leisure in America: Blessing or Curse?*, American Academy of Political and Social Science Monograph no. 4, 1960, p. 29.
5. R. Dubin, in a letter to the writer, 7 May 1963.
6. G. Friedmann, *The Anatomy of Work*, London: Heinemann, 1961, p. 152.
7. *Ibid.*, p. 153.
8. *Ibid.*, p. xvii.
9. J. Ellul, *The Technological Society*, London: Cape, 1965, pp. 400–402.
10. D. Riesman, 'Leisure and Work in Post-Industrial Society', in E. Larrabee and R. Meyersohn, (eds.), *Mass Leisure*, Glencoe: Free Press, 1958.
11. H. E. Barnes and O. M. Ruedi, *The American Way of Life*, New York: Prentice-Hall, 1950, p. 810.
12. H. Marcuse, *Eros and Civilization*, New York: Vintage Books, 1962, p. 178.
13. M. Vincent and J. Mayers, *New Foundations for Industrial Sociology*, Princeton: Van Nostrand, 1959, p. 423. After my text went to press, Kenneth Roberts' book *Leisure* (Longman, 1970) was published, in which he argues that leisure has become the basis of contemporary life. For my critical review of this book see *New Society*, 19 Nov. 1970.
14. F. Friedlander, 'Importance of Work Versus Nonwork Among Socially and Occupationally Stratified Groups', *Journal of Applied Psychology*, Dec. 1966.
15. H. L. Wilensky, 'Mass Society and Mass Culture: Interdependence?', *American Sociological Review*, April 1964.
16. P. Hollander, 'Leisure as an American and Soviet Value', *Social Problems*, Fall 1966.
17. B. B. Seligman, 'On Work, Alienation and Leisure', *American Journal of Economics and Sociology*, Oct. 1965.
18. K. Keniston, 'Social Change and Youth in America', *Daedalus*, Winter 1962.

10 IMPLICATIONS FOR SOCIAL POLICY

1. H. L. Wilensky, 'Work, Careers, and Social Integration', *International Social Science Journal*, No. 4, 1960, p. 546.

2. Thus 13% of a sample of local government electors thought that more should be done to provide leisure facilities in their areas, the proportion being exceeded only by those naming old people's welfare (16%) and housing matters (14%). (L. Moss and S. R. Parker, *The Local Government Councillor*, London: H.M.S.O., 1967, p. 219.)

3. *Daily Mirror*, 18 May 1964.

4. W. C. Sutherland, 'A Philosophy of Leisure', *Annals of the American Academy of Political and Social Science*, Sept. 1957.

5. J. C. Charlesworth, 'A Bold Program for Recreation', *Annals of the American Academy of Political and Social Science*, Sept. 1957.

6. E. Fromm, *The Sane Society*, London: Routledge, 1956, pp. 32, 361.

7. M. Harrington, *The Accidental Century*, London: Weidenfeld and Nicolson, 1966, p. 264.

8. A. Day, 'Leisure for Living', *Observer*, 17 May 1964. But in America workers 'determinedly chose, and collectively bargained for, more time away from the job.' (G. Soule, *What Automation Does to Human Beings*, London: Sidgwick, 1956, p. 94).

9. K. Denbigh, *Science, Industry and Social Policy*, Edinburgh: Oliver and Boyd, 1963, p. 25.

10. *Ibid.*, p. 45.

11. A. Vitomir, 'The Social Planning of Leisure', *International Social Science Journal*, No. 4, 1960, p. 581.

12. J. Dumazedier, *Toward a Society of Leisure*, London: Collier Macmillan, 1967, p. 230.

13. M. A. Fried, 'Is Work a Career?', *Trans-Action*, Sept.–Oct. 1966.

14. One optimistic estimate for Germany is that, assuming no increase in the 1968 level of gross domestic product, a $4\frac{1}{2}$% average annual growth rate of productivity could make possible by 1985 a halving of weekly hours of work and half the year as paid leave. But it seems more reasonable to expect that hours of work will continue to decline only slowly and that some groups, such as those whose unskilled labour is less needed or who are organized in strong trade unions, will gain more free time than others. (See H. L. Wilensky, 'The Uneven Distribution of Leisure', *Social Problems*, Summer 1961.)

15. G. Soule, *op. cit.*, p. 129.

16. H. A. Rhee, *Office Automation in Social Perspective*, Oxford: Blackwell, 1968, p. 215.

17. M. Bressler, 'Some Selected Aspects of American Sociology', *Annals of the American Academy of Political and Social Science*, Sept. 1961.

18. A. Willener, 'French Sociology and the Problem of Social Engineering', paper presented to the British Sociological Association Conference, London, 1967.

19. Ralph Glasser makes a similar point in stressing that there is no such thing now as an *unguided* mass opinion, if indeed there ever was. 'The problem for society is to ensure that the people or institutions exercising the "guidance" are socially responsible, and that they are motivated in the interests of transcendental values, not the expediency of commercial or power interests.' (*Leisure—Penalty or Prize?*, London: Macmillan, 1970, p. 208.) Apart from preferring some more substantial and humanistic adjective than 'transcendental', I entirely agree.

20. R. Aron, *Progress and Disillusion: the Dialectics of Modern Society*, London: Pall Mall Press, 1968, p. 106.

21. W. A. Faunce, 'Automation and Leisure', in H. B. Jacobson and J. S. Roucek, (eds.), *Automation and Society*, New York: Philosophical Library, 1959, p. 305.

22. N. Samuel, 'Prediction and Comparison in the Sociology of Leisure', paper presented to the British Sociological Association Conference, London, 1967.

Index

Abilities
  potential, 92–3, 97–8
  use of, 81, 83–4, 103, 106
Absenteeism, 67
Accountancy, 44, 80
Achievement, social, 22, 83, 113
Activities, 21, 29, 30, 38–40, 128, 135 (*and see* Leisure, Non-work, Work)
Activity, as dimension, 20–32 *passim*
Advertising, 60, 80, 128, 138
Agriculture, 34–5, 40, 54
Aldermen, 91, 94
Alienation, 99, 130, 141 (*and see* Work)
Almoning, 77, 80
America, 57, 60, 65, 73, 128, 131
Amusement (commercialized), 54–5, 114, 119
Anderson, J. M., 68, 148
Anderson, N., 145
Anthropology, 14, 33, 138
Apathy of workers, 13, 99
Aquinas, St Thomas, 35
Arendt, Hannah, 19, 39, 137, 144
Arensberg, C. M., 150
Aristotle, 123
Aron, Raymond, 61–2, 139, 147, 153
Arriens, Jan, 8
Art(s), 37, 57, 117
Artisans, 34
Artists, 19, 20
Ashton, H., 40, 146
Associations, voluntary, 67 (*and see* Organizations, non-work)
Australia, 69
Authoritarianism, 15
Authority, 46, 104
Automation, 11, 41, 53–4, 118–19, 131, 135–6, 140
Automobile industry, 53
Autonomy, 100, 117, 139
  in leisure, 138
  in work, 44, 50, 76–9, 81–2, 103, 105, 133

Bacon, Bill, 1
Baluchi, 40
Banking, 79–84, 105–7
Barnes, H. E., 145, 151
Basuto, 40
Bell, Daniel, 73, 149
Berger, Peter L., 51, 105, 146, 150
Bingo, 73
Blakelock, E. H., 147
Blau, Peter M., 75, 149
Blauner, Robert, 53, 146
Blomberg, W., 72, 149
Blum, Fred H., 66, 148
Boggs, T., 146
Bressler, M., 137, 153
Bricklayer, 45
Brightbill, Charles K., 21–2, 144–5
British Travel Association, 145, 147
Brown, Richard, 8
Burns, Tom, 76, 114, 150–1
Bushmen, 39
Business, 24, 88
  employees, 66, 71, 75–85, 107–8, 113, 121–2 (*and see* Executives)

Calvin, 35
Campanella, 36
Camping, 66
Capitalism, 47
Capitalists, 52
Casework, 46, 77, 90
Catholicism, 34–5, 86
Central life interest: *see* Life
Ceremonies, 38
Change, social, 14, 110, 130–2, 137, 141–2
Character, American, 72
Charlesworth, James, 129, 152
Child, John, 8
Child care (officers), 49, 80–5, 107
Children, 16, 26, 55, 60, 87–8, 91, 113
China, 57
Chivers, Terence, 8
Choice, 22, 117, 135, 143 (*and see* Occupation)
  leisure as, 27–9, 134, 138
Christianity, primitive, 34

Index

Index

Index